100 WAYS

TO MAKE YOUR BUSINESS A SUCCESS

A resource book for
small business managers

howtobooks

Neil Bromage

Published by How To Books Ltd,
3 Newtec Place, Magdalen Road,
Oxford OX4 1RE, United Kingdom.
Tel: (01865) 793806. Fax: (01865) 248780.
email: info@howtobooks.co.uk
http://www.howtobooks.co.uk

First edition 2003
Second edition 2005

British Library Cataloguing in Publication Data
A catalogue record for this book is available from the British
Library

Cover design by Baseline Arts Ltd, Oxford
Produced for How To Books by Deer Park Productions,
Tavistock
Typeset by PDQ Typesetting, Newcastle-under-Lyme, Staffs.
Printed and bound by Cromwell Press, Trowbridge, Wiltshire

NOTE: The material contained in this book is set out in good
faith for general guidance and no liability can be accepted
for loss or expense incurred as a result of relying in particular
circumstances on statements made in the book. The laws and
regulations are complex and liable to change, and readers should
check the current position with the relevant authorities before
making personal arrangements.

Contents

Introduction

Running a business is never easy. More often than not it's a roller-coaster ride through a range of hazards and difficulties. But one thing is for sure: life will rarely, if ever, be dull. This book has one single purpose – **to help you build a better business.**

Here you will find a wide-ranging resource of valuable information for anyone involved in running a business, wherever they are on the roller-coaster. This book contains not only basic information that is all too often overlooked when we are busy taking care of business, but also useful insights into just about every area of business management.

I have written this book in what I feel is an easy-to-understand manner. It is based on the advice I've been giving through the Business Link network over a number of years and follows those frequently asked questions that business managers throw up, together with advice gathered from some of the leading lights in the business community.

But if there's one piece of advice I feel it's necessary to give to would-be business owners and entrepreneurs it's that you must enjoy it. If you're not enjoying running your business you can't expect to do it well. More often than not the high points on the ride will more than compensate for the lows as the excitement of reaching a goal brings a surge of adrenalin which drives us all forward.

There are many people who have in some way contributed to this book, not least of all the many well-known business people who have kindly given me their time. Kate Santon, in editing it, has put it into a format of easy-to-follow sections for which I'm tremendously grateful; her patience in dealing with a writer/journo whose attitude to deadlines is to work right up to them could not go without mention and thanks. Nikki Read at How To Books can't be allowed to escape. She has been guilty of constantly encouraging me with ideas over a number of years and has always provided a listening ear, which has finally led to this book appearing. Thank you, Nikki.

But after twenty years on that roller-coaster of business life I couldn't fail to mention my silent co-producer, my wife Jackie. She has been there through all those ups and downs. But more importantly, for twenty years and more she has encouraged the writer in me. Without her love and support this book wouldn't have been written.

I hope that as you read this resource book you will find it useful and valuable in helping you to build a better business.

Neil Bromage

Author: What does it take to succeed in business today?

John Oliver OBE was the Chief Executive of Leyland Trucks until 1998 and now runs Optima Personnel Services and Team Enterprise Solutions.

'You have to have intelligence, courage, endurance and hard work. If you're starting from scratch you also need imagination, entrepreneurial flare and a lot of luck! However, as business grows, you'll also need to develop a natural empathy with and for people. Those who succeed nowadays in medium to large concerns are increasingly seen to have acquired an aliation for employee interest which results in a motivated workforce.'

Sir John Harvey-Jones,
'Well, luck and I think probably the most important thing is the ability to listen. You can't just do your own thing. You've got to listen to your employees, you've got to listen to your customers or sometimes listen to old farts like me.'

Section One

Making Your Business Work

$$\left(1\right)$$

Ideas –
The Lifeblood of Business

Without a constant flow of ideas most businesses will fail. But ideas can be good and bad. So how do you generate and assess them in order to begin a new business or grow an existing one?

Ideas are vital to develop new or existing products or services or even to take that first step into a new business. In fact wherever you are in the business life cycle you'll need lots of ideas if your business is to thrive.

Generating ideas is the first step and some of the questions you should be asking are 'What if?', 'How?' and 'Why?' Try looking at how you can change existing products or services to meet an unmet need, an existing need in a different, more convenient way or to improve quality or service. Be observant and on the lookout for emerging trends and expanding market niches.

During this process, employ any technique you can think of, including brainstorming. It's often hard to find the time for this but it's well worth doing. Focus on your consumer and market, not on your product – there's no point in making something better if no one needs or wants it in the first place.

Once you have a shortlist of ideas it's time to start assessing them as viable business opportunities. This means devoting time and effort to assessment, research, development and planning.

Talk about your product or service with prospective customers. Is there really demand for your offerings? If so, how strong? How price sensitive? What sets you apart from your competition?

Research everything you can about your target market and competition. Who are they, how are they structured, how long have they been in business, what are their respective market shares, what sets you apart? Are price wars common? If so, you may have too much competition. Are there only one or two big players and no little ones? Look for markets where there is healthy competition between product or service providers but where profit margins are reasonable. Work out your expenses and how much revenue you need to generate to break even. Then project realistically how much you need to make a profit.

Ideas really are the lifeblood of any business and vital to its long-term success. Try to set time aside for developing new ideas on a regular basis and your business will not only survive, but prosper too.

Researching Your Ideas

When the going gets tough effective market research can provide a real edge against the competition. There are three areas that can reap rewards for businesses hungry for success.

Market research is vital for any business as it determines whether or not people will want to buy what you have to offer. It can provide valuable information for your business plan and strengthen your case if you are going to the bank for money. The three main areas of research worth exploring are:

1. Your customer base

When carrying out market research on your potential customer base ask yourself who your clients are. How many are there? Where are they? How can they be contacted? Who controls their decision-making process?

2. Your customer demands

You should also consider what your prospective clients actually want: what services do they most need? When are they likely to want your services? How much would they be willing to pay you? Can you package your services in a particularly attractive manner?

3. The competition

You can't complete effective research without also considering your competitors. Who are they? If there is no competition, why not? What are the competition's strengths and weaknesses? What types of indirect competition exist?

Much of this information can often be found at the following sources:

- **Libraries**: Reference libraries are particularly useful; the commercial section often contains reports on various market sectors and competitors. You will also find directories of organisations by industry type, which could be a valuable resource.
- **Trade associations**: most of these have specialist libraries on market sectors.
- **Trade publications**: magazines or news-sheets can give you up-to-date information on the movements of the industry and your competitors.
- **Exhibitions and conferences**: make contacts, promote yourself and examine the competition.
- **Telephone directories**: *Yellow Pages* and *Thomson*'s list all your local competition. You can check out those from other areas at the reference library.
- **Companies house**: for details on limited companies and copies of their audited accounts.

The more time you spend on market research the more likely you are to tailor your services to the needs of your clients. And if you are selling what your clients want, you are more likely to develop a successful business.

Business Plans to Get Ahead

A good business plan is critical to the success of your business – and so is the need to update it frequently. Here are some of the vital ingredients.

Life can be chaotic when you are starting or running a business and the day-to-day management issues can often force long-term planning on to the back burner. But allowing short-term problems to distract you from long-term goals will not help your business to grow.

Having a business plan and sticking to it is one way to ensure the business stays on track. It is not, however, merely something which satisfies the bank. A business plan is a tool for measuring performance on an ongoing basis, and it's good business practice.

A good business plan should be ambitious but realistic. It's pointless setting targets for sales or expenses that cannot be met. It should include a summary of the business and its marketplace, the past (if the business has one), management details including experience, description of the product or service and how it will be marketed and sold, financial analysis – which should include profit and loss accounts, cashflow forecasts and balance sheets. Remember that a business plan is also a selling tool. You will need to get across to readers just what is interesting about your business and exactly why anyone would want to invest in it. An ideal format would be between three and ten pages drawing out all the important points. It's also worth having the plan looked at by an independent expert before showing it to potential financiers.

When the plan for your business or project is written it should enable you to compare targets against actual performance. This will help you to monitor the progress of the business on a regular basis. It may also give early indications of the need to reassess the situation and even rewrite the plan to take account of new issues.

When used as both a planning and measurement tool a well written business plan will drive the business forward in a positive manner. After all, you wouldn't dream of setting off to drive around the world without a road map, would you?

Freelancing for Business

Freelancing is a great way to do business. And as the business world adapts to ever increasing change more people are finding that freelancing can provide a lucrative income and improved quality of life.

Successful freelancers operate within wide-ranging occupational environments. A website designer might choose to freelance, along with PR consultants, artists, writers and journalists, sales or marketing specialists or bricklayers and plasterers. In fact anyone who chooses to work on an ad hoc contract basis is a freelancer.

The simple fact is that freelancing is more about choosing a lifestyle than anything else. It offers the opportunity to say yes or no to the work you do and when you do it. Some freelancers work for six months of the year and then holiday for the remainder. Others choose to work the same patterns as their employed counterparts.

Freelancers are not employees of anyone and must actively seek out their own work, negotiate the terms and conditions of the project and complete it to the satisfaction of the client. The pay is usually better – a good freelancer can generally do much better than the average employee doing the same work, though it takes time to develop a reputation that people are prepared to pay a premium for.

But there are also things that you may find less attractive. For instance, in most occupations you'll need to be prepared for isolation and loneliness. You'll have to chase payments – not everyone is going to pay you merely because you send an invoice. A good proportion of your time will be spent cold-calling, selling and marketing yourself. If you don't like doing that freelancing may not be for you.

Networking is probably is one of the most important aspects of the freelance life. Much of this can be done on the telephone – you will be surprised at the relationships you can build up without ever meeting someone. Similarly, keeping good records and accounts is vital for the freelancer – you'll have to pay tax just the same as everyone else!

Freelancing can be a great life but has the same challenges and opportunities as any other business – so make sure it's right for you before turning your back on the security of employment.

SWOT Up On Your Business

Success in business is all to do with good planning. Here is another way of looking at your plan which will set your business off in the right direction.

There are many reasons why a business plan is a valuable tool when it comes to managing your business. Most fundamentally, it helps you 'set your sail' in the direction you want your business to go. Rather than drifting along aimlessly, being tugged this way and that by random currents and puffs of wind, a business plan helps you steer a predetermined course and stay on track.

A good starting point when thinking about the elements of your business plan is to carry out a SWOT analysis. What are your business's Strengths, Weaknesses, Opportunities and Threats?

The strengths you identify will become the foundation for your competitive focus. Think of ways to exploit them as they will set you apart from your competition. For example, you may be particularly good with people: use this talent in the customer service aspects of your business to distinguish you from the competition. Similarly, by identifying weaknesses you can plan for ways to compensate for them.

The opportunities you identify become the cornerstones for your business development. What opportunities exist that you can exploit in the next twelve months to develop your business? The threats become the foundation for your contingency planning. By recognising threats before they become a reality, you will be better placed to implement contingency plans and ride out the storm.

Once armed with your SWOT inventory you can begin to refine your thinking in terms of coming up with an overall strategy for your business.

Finally, bear in mind that a business plan is just that, a plan, it's not carved in stone. Be flexible and make changes as circumstances and priorities alter. Work with your plan and treat it as a living, breathing, organic part of your business.

By constantly keeping your plan in mind when making decisions you can rest comfortably, knowing you are steering your business in the direction *you* want it to go.

Setting Rates

Setting rates for the work you do can often be difficult. How do you estimate how long a job will take? How do you decide if your rates should be hourly or by the project?

Wrestling with how much to charge for the services you provide is an age-old dilemma that many businesses struggle with daily.

Charging by the hour is probably the simplest method. Keep track of the hours you have worked on a project, as many employers will want a detailed breakdown so that they know they are getting their money's worth. If the project is small, won't last very long and is very specific, then charging by the hour is probably your best option. It's also a good option when you're unclear about the real scope of a project and feel it could mushroom into something that takes you twice as long.

Charging by the project is the best option when it is long term or clearly defined. The client then knows what to expect up front, and you have an idea in your head of how long it should take you to complete the project.

To set a rate for a project, you need to assess it accurately. Decide what the project entails, what problems you need to solve and how long you think it will take to do a thorough job. Don't forget to add in some time for unseen problems – few projects ever go exactly according to plan. Then decide what your hourly rate will be. Only you know your experience in the field, your monetary needs, and your expertise for each individual project. Use all these criteria to set a rate that is fair to you and fair to your client, having thoroughly checked out the rates of your competitors.

Setting rates and bidding on projects takes some under-standing and assessment. You need to understand and assess the projects, and your needs and talents. There is no perfect answer; bidding an hourly rate or by project really depends on you, and the project.

Just keep on bidding, and those projects will come your way.

Choosing
Professional Advisers

A good accountant, lawyer or business consultant can make or break your business. So how do you make sure you choose the right advisers?

Most businesses need advisers of one sort or another in order to function properly. Some will see an accountant just once a year whilst others will need a range of professionals for legal, tax planning or management accounting advice. These are close relationships with each adviser knowing the very smallest detail of your business. A bad adviser can wreck your business.

Whilst most advisers belong to professional bodies, these will tell you little apart from whether the individual is licensed to practise. Personal knowledge is useful but try to avoid using personal friends, as this can often be a hindrance rather than an advantage. It can also ruin a good friendship. Try to get a personal recommendation from someone whose judgement you trust. Ask other businesses who they use and why.

It's also important to define the needs of your business and be clear in your mind about these, as it's easy to be sold services you don't actually need. If, for instance, your business is highly specialised you may well require a specialised service which you can't find locally. Distance can be a barrier but modern technology means that many of these are being gradually eroded.

Look for firms with a reputation in your area or industry and at who is hiring new people and what their specialities are. Approach a few firms at the same time to find out which one really wants your business. Remember, you're paying the bill and if they are not willing to make an effort to get your business they are probably not worth using.

You could try out a firm before giving them all your business, though this will be easier with certain types of work – legal for instance, where work is normally done on an ad hoc basis. You may also have two firms providing accountancy help – one for year-end accounts and another for taxation advice. After all, we are all more effective and sharper when we're in competition with someone else!

Always remember that these advisers will be an essential part of your business. You want them to be as keen as you are.

Niche Markets

Niche markets can be very lucrative for small businesses. But how do you identify them and assess whether they are right for your business?

Smaller businesses often have a very focused strategy, operating in a small part of a market with great success. This enables them to compete with larger organisations and achieve a level of protection against competition.

The advantage of operating in a niche is that it gives you the opportunity to become a strong supplier in a small market. But it's important to identify your niche correctly with sound judgments based on thorough research.

- ◆ Analyse other businesses operating in your market and the products or services they offer. Do their products or services attract a wide range of customers or just a few targeted ones?

- ◆ Use this analysis to decide what degree of specialisation your product or service calls for. Will operating in a niche mean alterations to your product or service? Can you offer flexible service solutions?

- ◆ Identify areas where customers' needs aren't already being met and look for a competitive edge by adding features or offering a value-added service that isn't currently available.

♦ Conduct research to see if there is a group of customers that your competitors are failing to reach and consider how your product or service could be updated or adapted to attract them.

♦ Explore how your customers buy from your competitors. Can your product or service be sold in a different way – over the Internet or through a mail order catalogue?

Once you've completed this analysis use the information to identify customers that have things in common and things that make them different from others buying in that market. Then create a profile of these customers and use this as the basis of market research to ensure the niche is viable.

Action checklist

♦ Do your research. Go to trade shows, collect competitors' catalogues and look at trade magazines to find out what's already on the market.

♦ Talk to potential customers and find out what they want.

Niche markets can indeed be lucrative, but if you operate in one keep a close eye on its growth. Always remember that many larger markets have grown out of niches.

Finding Clients

Finding clients and keeping them happy is the key to successful self-employment. Here are a few easy tips to keep your customers smiling.

Most businesses will tell you that word of mouth soon carries the good news to others and leads to more business and bigger fees simply because customers will pay for quality service. Happy customers mean you have to be prepared to go the extra mile and work that little bit harder.

Finding them

Keep a record of where your new customers come from – was it from a recommendation by an existing customer or did they see you at an exhibition? This is vital information; it helps you focus your resources on communication channels that work for you. Experiment with low cost ways of creating customers. For example, visiting exhibitions, sending out press releases, mail shots, etc. Generally the most direct methods are the most effective. So pick up the phone rather than place an ad.

Use your existing customers to help you create new ones by asking for a reference or personal recommendation. Be passionate about your business: customers like passion and energy. Demonstrating genuine interest in a customer's business is very persuasive and attractive, and a common complaint from the customers of service providers is that 'they do not show any real interest in our business'.

Find out something about potential customers beforehand and appear informed. Be persistent when chasing customers. Remember, buyers expect to be courted and often make you work to get their business.

Keeping them

Remember people buy people, not products, so...

- Pay attention. Consider the person you are with as the only one in the universe who matters.
- Don't talk – listen. It's better to laugh at somebody else's funny story than tell your own.
- Empathise. Watch body language to assess how the other person is feeling. Try to match those feelings.
- Be enthusiastic. Use your face and body to convey emotion. If you don't show you are interested, people feel as if they are talking to a brick wall.
- Be approachable and not at all aggressive.
- Be authentic. Be honest and straightforward with people at all times. Honesty builds trust, trust creates customers.

Finding and keeping clients is vital and should form an integral part of your planning if you want to grow your business.

Researching Your Target Companies

Time spent researching target companies can reap dividends. Here is some advice on how to gather information about the businesses you want to work with.

If knowledge is power, then researching a target company can give you a much better understanding of what they do and help you to prepare a successful bid or sales pitch.

You may also find other companies in the same field that you didn't know existed who can offer you similar opportunities. You may discover that those opportunities fit your needs perfectly. Either way, a little time spent researching these target companies can save you trials and tribulations later on and give your business a real competitive edge over the rest of the field.

What should you look for when you research a company? There are a wide variety of helpful details you can discover. Are they a subsidiary of another company, or a parent company? What are their long-term goals? Who are their customers? How are they managed? Do they look successful, and if so, why?

Then you can also find out how long they have been in business, how many people work for the organisation and what products and services they offer. You can read financial reports, which can reveal all sorts of useful information including what they predict their growth will be. You can also look at their major competitors. All of this can be invaluable as the more you know about a company, the more you can match your knowledge and experience to their needs and tailor your proposal accordingly.

How do you research a company? There are many online resources available to anyone looking for company information. Try searching for their corporate website on a search engine such as Google, Excite or Yahoo!. If they have a site, it will probably show up in a search of their name. Alternatively, local libraries can also be helpful.

Researching a company does take some time, but it's time well spent. Learn more about them and what they do, and you'll give yourself an edge against all those other prospective bidders who didn't take the time to do their homework.

11

How to Sell Professional Services

Many self-employed professionals love the freedom of their position but hate trying to sell their services. Here's some advice to help all those reluctant professionals who need to sell to clients.

Research shows that fear of selling is one of the greatest barriers to business success and, often, professionals are the worst of all. But whether you are a film technician or an accountant you still have to sell to keep the business coming in.

There are techniques which will help you to become successful at selling yourself. You don't have to turn into some sort of sharp-suited Arthur Daley – just do some preparation and think about your services from the customer's point of view.

Before you go into a business meeting spend some time:

- Listing the main features of your services – speed of delivery, quality, price, etc.
- Clarifying what makes you different from your competitors.
- Identifying the benefits your service will bring to the

client's business.

- Finding out as much as possible about the sort of person and organisation you will be meeting.
- Identifying reasons why they might not want your product and how you might respond to them.

Most importantly, think in terms of what the client needs and wants rather than what you are trying to sell them.

Once you get into the meeting you need to establish your credentials and the particular benefits of your services as quickly as possible. Your credentials will include you and your team – the people who will deliver the product or service; their expertise – skills, experience, etc.; what differentiates you from your competition; examples of other people who use your product or service, and in doing so endorse it.

Remember to explain how the client's business will benefit from using your services. Will it make them more efficient, save money or get more customers? Finally, and most importantly, look at how it will improve their bottom line.

Watch out if the client asks you more about competitors and their products. Don't rubbish the opposition; it doesn't look very professional. Just concentrate on the differences that will be of particular benefit to the client's business.

Always have a debrief after the meeting. Make some notes of what went down well with the client and where you went wrong. Then you can improve your selling technique next time round.

Checking Out a Prospect

You have found that new customer, but providing credit facilities can be a risky but necessary business. Here are some tips on checking out a prospect's creditworthiness.

Whatever the value of your products or services, the likelihood is that at some stage you'll be faced with deciding whether or not to offer credit to a customer you don't know very well. Checking them out could prevent a future bad debt.

Initially, it's always worth listening to the grapevine. People talk and nothing travels faster than bad news. Talk to other suppliers with whom these prospects may have had dealings. Even talk to your competition if you are on good terms with them. After all, you would reciprocate – wouldn't you?

Bank references can be of some value, though this can often be limited. They may say something along the lines of 'should prove good for normal business engagements/ credit of xxx pounds a month'. But if the report says 'Your figures are larger than we would normally expect to see,' this indicates that the amount you were enquiring about may put a strain on the account holder's resources. Be wary of references reading 'Resources fully committed' or 'Unable to speak for your figures'.

Trade references can also be of value though this is, again, limited because shaky businesses often try to keep on the right side of a handful of suppliers for trade reference purposes.

When taking references you can ask some or all of the following questions:

- Are you associated with the company at all?

- How long have you traded with them?

- Are you currently trading with them?

- What is the maximum credit you have extended to this firm in one month?

- What are your payment terms?

- Compared with these terms, are the customer's payments prompt, reasonable, slow or poor?

- Have you had to take any final collection action in the last six months?

- Is there any other relevant information you think we should know?

Finally, trust your instincts. They are often right.

$$\bigcirc\!\!\!13$$

Branding Your Business

Creating a strong brand for your business can set you apart from the pack and lay foundations for future growth.

If you think only big corporations need to think about brand names, think again. Your brand says a lot about you and your business, and that's as true for a one-person, home-based operation as it is for a multinational conglomerate.

Your brand is more than just the logo on your letterhead and business cards. It's your corporate identity. An effective brand tells the world who you are, what you do and how you do it, while at the same time establishing your relevance to and credibility with your prospective customers.

If your brand has a high perceived value, you enjoy many advantages over your competition, especially when it comes to pricing. For instance, people are prepared to pay more for items with recognised brands on them – this is perceived value as a result of effective brand promotion resulting in very high brand awareness.

When your brand is well known in this way it creates further awareness of your unique selling proposition within your market place. This can help to make your sales force (even if that's a sales force of one – you) more effective and efficient. Imagine if you didn't have to spend the first 50% of your time with a new prospect explaining who you are, what you do and how you do it because your brand had already communicated that for you.

When you create your brand, you need to keep the who, what and how firmly in mind but also use the brand to establish your relevance to your target market and build credibility with that market. Start by creating a mission statement. What is the mission of your business? What are your core values? When you know these you can begin thinking about creating a brand that reinforces and supports your aims.

A properly descriptive brand and high brand awareness in your target market will allow you to more easily introduce a wider range of products and services. Your brand has already pre-sold *you*. Your job is then to sell your products and services.

$$\left(14\right)$$

Building Your Brand

Successful branding is one of the keys to creating a strong business that can flourish whatever the climate. Building your brand is not complicated, but simply means understanding your brand and customers.

Convincing your customers that your brand is the best will help you command a stronger position in the marketplace. To do this you need to consider the underlying implications of successful branding.

Generally speaking, brands are either primary or secondary, which will affect how you market them. *Primary* brands are the main products or services marketed by your business and *secondary* brands are additions or extensions to the main product.

Paying attention to the following will help you to build a stronger brand:

◆ **Image:** look for qualities your customers appreciate and work hard to maintain your reputation – it's always easier to lose a good reputation than it is to build one.

- **Quality:** customer satisfaction becomes self-perpetuating so be sure to maintain standards so that the customer has continued faith in your brand.

- **Customer commitment:** loyalty works both ways so be long-term and consistent in your planning.

- **Pricing:** this is part of a customer's perception of value. Higher prices are often equated with higher value.

- **High profile marketing:** keep your brand in the public eye as much as possible, thereby maintaining customer awareness.

- **Packaging:** this can often have a significant impact on sales and unique packaging can be a part of the whole brand identity. The name of your brand can be crucial to its success. It should have universal appeal and be capable of crossing cultural barriers.

Be aware that your competitors will quickly copy and improve on your good ideas so focus on the competitive edge you can offer and maintain. If you succeed in making your brand synonymous with a product group or general service (as with the name 'Hoover', now used to describe all vacuum cleaners) you may be able to create a perceived value which remains constant, even in a fluctuating market.

Understanding your customers' needs and their perception of quality will be vital to this process. Remember that good, consistent marketing will encourage customers to accept your brand as an essential part of their everyday lives.

How to Leapfrog Your Competitors

Keeping a jump ahead of the competition means knowing precisely what they are up to. Here are some tips to help you stay one, if not several, leaps ahead.

Few businesses keep tabs on competitors, yet such knowledge can give you a distinctive competitive edge. Building a file on them, looking at everything from the customer's viewpoint and asking suppliers and employees what they know about them can be worthwhile.

Remember, before starting to gather information, that your competitors will come in two forms, direct and indirect – the latter being those selling the same product but in different ways.

Build a profile
Ask yourself what products and services they offer. Do they overlap with yours? What customer needs and wants are they satisfying? What is their unique selling proposition? How do they position themselves? Are they the Savoy or a McDonald's? Is their mind-set corner shop, high street franchise or old establishment? Are they exclusive and high-priced or a dime-a-dozen? Are they as passionate and knowledgeable as you?

How do they market themselves? Where do they advertise? What sales channels do they use – retail, direct mail, Internet, wholesale? What is their sales literature like? How can you make yours stand out in comparison? How good are their employees? Should you be considering enticing them over to you?

Are they growing, level pegging or declining? If so, why? Use the Internet to get hold of credit reports on them. Find out how many employees they have, and what they do.

Develop a strategy

Once you have all this information, analyse their strengths and weaknesses and relate them to your own, asking how each one affects you. And remember, their strengths are your threats, their weaknesses your opportunities. Are your strengths good enough to lure people away from the competition – or even to keep existing customers? Could your weaknesses be driving people away?

This kind of research and analysis will throw up lots of new opportunities. Acting on your findings will keep you ahead of your field. But remember, you don't have to be streets ahead — in a race, it's enough to win by as little as a nose.

Better By Design

Here is advice for all those who think design is merely a question of getting a new letterhead...

Today's business world is fast moving and ultra competitive. Competition is intense and customers expect better products and services. But products often don't last long in the marketplace. Consequently, businesses need to create, develop and differentiate constantly in order to compete and move forward. Design is an integral part of this process, and one that can help them to win new business.

Design helps businesses to compete as it enables marketing messages to be made visible and understood. The most successful businesses have a culture of creativity that has become an integral part of their organisation, improving production, design, sales and marketing, and even finance.

Everything in a business is affected by design, from staff work-wear to packaging, corporate literature to technology and manufacturing. The impact of a corporate website, for instance, can be crucial in winning business as it encourages a feeling of security in your customers and suppliers alike.

Increased sales and profit margins can also be generated by design. Better products will obviously be more attractive and therefore generate more sales. But better designed manufacturing processes or service operations which match the flexible requirements of the marketplace will save time and money. Reduced manufacturing and warranty costs will increase your profits and easier servicing will increase the satisfaction of your customers and increase sales.

Improving your image through better design will give more people the confidence to do business with you, but understanding what customers want is vital. Look at how Orange have changed the way mobile phones are sold, or how Dyson wrestled the vacuum cleaner market away from more established manufacturers. Both have been achieved using design.

Investing in design to grow your business works, the evidence is all around us — so go on, be really creative...

$$\left(\,17\,\right)$$

Profit From Ideas

New ideas are not just for the start of a business. Here's how to use them to improve your bottom line.

Product development and innovation are the lifeblood of business. To succeed it's essential to have new ideas that will differentiate your business from its competitors. All products have a certain life cycle and, just like wallpaper, they can quickly become out of date and in need of change.

Change is not only good, it's important. Where change does not occur competitors will sweep in and your business could lose the competitive advantage you have spent years building up.

But innovation and change are not only for larger companies; it applies equally to the smaller business. They, in fact, have much to offer in this area, with their flexibility, energy, willingness to embrace new ideas, ability to hear what the customer is saying and above all to get to the market more quickly. In today's dot.com society that is frequently the most important factor.

Innovation is about ideas, and using them to the best advantage of the business. Ideas can come from anywhere and anybody. Everyone has ideas, though some people don't always recognise this. For a business to become truly innovative management needs to listen to everyone in the organisation, and where necessary actually ask people for their thoughts.

This may well mean a cultural change throughout the business and encouraging people to share ideas. This can be done everywhere – in product development, service and production – but will involve getting the right balance of creative, technical and managerial skills.

To profit from ideas and become truly innovative evaluate your current position within the marketplace, customers' needs and demands and the effectiveness of your products/services to fulfil these. The more value that can be added to the product or service the more likely it is that sustainable competitive advantage can be developed. This is the key to long-term profit.

Remember, only one company can be the cheapest: all the others must be innovative.

Strategic Alliances

Many hands make light work – 'team' businesses can offer a better way to compete in the marketplace.

Most people running small businesses would prefer to remain small and manageable. That does not mean that at times they shouldn't think big, if only for a limited time.

Businesses are waking up to the fact that strategic alliances or partnerships can provide platforms to bid for larger projects or take on more interesting work. Where, for example, a small business does not have the required capacity to take on a new contract, or a larger firm needs to enlist more specialist help, forming a strategic alliance can enable them to compete.

Businesses who build relationships like this will be better placed to gain a significant competitive edge over their rivals. It's more than a 'virtual' business and less than merging two businesses, and can offer enhanced reputation, improved effectiveness and lower risk.

Building successful partnerships with others who may be competitors takes time and trust but the benefits are worthwhile. Imagine, for instance, being able to fire your main supplier with sufficient enthusiasm for a particular project that they agree to combine their skills and experience to help you win the project. You immediately get the benefit of their improved purchasing power.

A successful alliance needs:

- ◆ Genuine commitment from both organisations.
- ◆ A firm understanding of what is expected.
- ◆ Suitably trained, capable people to carry out the job.
- ◆ Sufficient resources to ensure success.
- ◆ Patience to tackle obstacles – there will be some.
- ◆ Open communication.

Whilst there are clearly a number of legitimate concerns such as a lack of partner commitment, loss of control and potential loss of customers, these are fears which should not put anyone off exploring a strategic alliance which can improve their position.

You may find that a prospective partner already has a close working relationship with another company – perhaps one of your competitors. This is reassuring because the other party will know what is expected, and disconcerting because of the confidential information you may have to share. You could reconsider the amount of information passed on or alternatively simply disclose it and clearly indicate to your partner that you possess that most critical of ingredients for a successful partnership – trust!

Teaming up with another business, freelancer or contractor really can help you to enhance your business in a way that suits you and will also provide a tremendous amount of flexibility to allow you to continue doing your own thing.

How to Use Management Consultants

Management consultants can provide an independent eye on your business. Making sure the relationship and brief are right from the outset is key to good results.

The effective use of management consultants isn't simply about making a financial commitment. It also requires a substantial commitment of time as keeping fully in touch with the progress of the assignment is vital if you are to get the most out of it.

Perhaps the single most important factor in ensuring a successful outcome is in preparing a good brief for the consultant. Working together, you should plan exactly what it is you're hoping to achieve from having the consultant working in the heart of your business.

Having an agreed programme and timescale is equally important and also necessary for cost effectiveness. Regular progress meetings with the consultant will keep you fully briefed on how the programme is going and enable you to assess any adjustments that may be needed.

It will also be necessary to involve your management and staff in providing input whilst the consultant is carrying out investigative research into the business, and then when it comes to implementing his recommendations. This will enable staff to take ownership of the recommendations and have an interest in the results.

As a general rule consultants are usually most effective when the work is done on the client's premises. This will mean providing suitable office space and administrative support for them.

The consultant's final report (if it has been agreed that one will be produced) needs to be in a format that is beneficial to you and written in a way you and your staff can understand and use. If necessary, ask to see a draft report that you can discuss before it is finalised. Where any contentious or confidential issues are raised you might ask for these to be set out separately, rather than in the report itself.

Asking the consultant to help with implementation of the report may be considered additional work, so remember to get a written quotation of fees.

You are paying the bills, and if you're not happy you should tell the consultants and explain why. Remember that good management consultancy can help your business to grow more effectively.

20

Upsizing – Moving On From Freelancing

There comes a time in the life of most freelancers when the lure of building their business into something bigger seems very attractive. So how do you upsize and make that move into the real business world?

Being a freelancer can be quite isolating – mainly because that's exactly what most freelancers choose. It's a little like swimming without getting your hair wet – you're never fully immersed in the environment. When the decision is taken to upsize and begin to really build, rather then maintain, your business, it becomes necessary to totally submerge yourself.

One of the first considerations is whether there is sufficient work. Can you see other opportunities where contracts can be acquired? Is there potential for creating strategic alliances with someone in an allied field in order to spin off each other? Or will a marketing campaign bring in new work? Ultimately, if there isn't more work you can't expand.

Your workspace will need serious review. Can you continue at home – that's where most freelancers work – or is there a need to move into new premises, buy more equipment and take on staff? All of this costs more than is often thought and you need to know how it will be financed.

You will undoubtedly need the support of a good banker, and not just in financial terms. This needs to be someone you can really talk to and get advice from. Try to be discerning here, talk to a few managers before deciding who you think you can get on with, remembering that all business is about relationships.

So, you've checked out your market, assessed your resources, made sure you've got the finances in place and written a great business plan. Is it time to dive into the pool? Perhaps. If you've got a survival plan that will make it easier. If you've got contracted work in place that will be very helpful. Ultimately there is only you who can make the final decision but if you feel any doubt whatsoever it's probably best to wait a while. If not, and your confidence is rising with every phone call, then go for it!

Outsourcing

To do, or not to do, that is the question. Small and medium-sized businesses can achieve more by doing less – here's how to achieve a competitive edge through outsourcing.

The path to growth is often difficult for small and medium-sized enterprises (SMEs). At some point most will find themselves in the classic conundrum of either being under-manned or under-financed and having their growth unrealised as a result.

With the constant need to cut costs outsourcing has gathered pace in recent years. It has also provided the means to bring a lot of good business ideas to fruition.

There are a variety of reasons for outsourcing, including improved efficiency, cost reductions, and increased flexibility. Situations are familiar, ranging from high-tech start-ups which are unable to raise funds or risk manufacturing their products to companies with cyclical sales, making production planning difficult and expensive.

Small business provides particularly good examples of the opportunities available for successful outsourcing, as the need for managers to be good sales people, administrators or receptionists whilst using the skills specific to their 'real' role is ever present.

Every business has core functions or competencies which represent where their profit comes from. It's the product they make or service they perform. Everything outside this function is secondary and generally capable of being done by someone else.

American outsourcing guru Michael F. Corbett offers a useful test for identifying core competencies:

- If starting today would you do it yourself?
- Would other companies hire you to do it for them?

If it is a core competency the answer to both questions will be yes.

At the start of the 1990s, 50% of the UK's total output was outsourced in some way. Traditionally this was in areas such as catering, cleaning and security but in more recent times this has extended into sales and marketing, facilities management and telephone answering. The fact is that it's possible to outsource almost anything.

The 'make or buy' decision has now been replaced by 'to do or not to do', but in the future the question will not be 'should we outsource?' but 'how do we best outsource?'. It is something every business should consider.

Virtual Teams

Working together in large offices is becoming a thing of the past as the Internet makes 'virtual working' more viable. Here is some advice for those businesses wanting to grow 'virtually'.

What is a typical virtual team?

A virtual team is a group of individuals working in different locations, often from home, either as freelancers or employees. Groups sometimes come together for a specific project and can allow you to grow your business without the headache of taking on bigger premises and all the related costs.

How will it work?

There are several issues to consider when forming a virtual team. What is its legal structure? Who takes the customer's order and who is legally responsible? How are decisions reached? Who is the boss? What is people's status: full- or part-time employees; sub-contractors or freelancers? How are they paid or rewarded? How are profits split? Does the client see a single entity or a group of individual talents?

Most virtual teams will come together from people who already know each other and perhaps have complementary skills which can be used to enhance each others' businesses. But where this is not the case some checks need to be made to ensure that virtual team members are of the appropriate standards.

Pitfalls

Communication is vital – you need to know when team members are sick or on holiday so you can arrange cover. The lack of human contact can lead to feelings of isolation. Be available to listen, and use the phone without counting the cost. Audio or videoconferencing can be effective for team briefings and bringing members together. Alternatively, set up an extranet with a chat room to keep members informed of group issues and to give scope for lighter gossip. Get the team together for regular face-to-face meetings. Have mechanisms to allow people to let off steam or air grievances.

Decide in advance how you will reach consensus on group issues. Team members must work in the same way, so give clear guidelines to ensure that work is handled consistently.

Virtual teams can save you money and help you to grow your business, while at the same time allowing employees or freelancers to spend more time at home with their families. They are the way of the future.

The Virtual Office

It's work, Jim, but not as we know it! The pros and cons of working from home.

In the past businesses that operated from home were often seen as part-time, and not treated as serious. Today, however, they are seen as the future for many individuals and companies. Improved communications tools mean that it's possible to work from almost anywhere. A PC in a spare bedroom enables businesses to communicate with the whole of the world instantly and the small owner/manager to talk to the CEO or president of a major worldwide company.

Unless a public front is essential – to sell products or services for instance – working from home is an alternative. Telephonists, sales people, administrative support and executive staff can all work efficiently at home providing the appropriate systems are in place.

Working from home has attractions for people and companies alike. For the individual, the convenience, improved working environment and removal of unnecessary travelling are all big gains. Walking straight into the office half an hour earlier, having spent an extra ten minutes over breakfast may help you to get more work done. Coupled with the ability to take a ten minute 'quality break' sitting in the garden, this sounds idyllic. For this to happen it's important to ensure that workspace is properly organised and where possible away from the rest of the home. Friends and family also need to understand that a person is working – just because they are at home in a pair of shorts doesn't mean they're on holiday.

For the company, remote working is becoming an increasingly attractive alternative to providing expensive offices. As the idea of the virtual office gathers pace employers are seeing the benefits of reduced overheads and more effective, happier staff. There are also savings on fuel and travelling expenses which add to the bottom line. Home working provides the opportunity of re-assessing operating methods. The 'new economy' is rapidly being made up of businesses that operate globally from very small bases, and the traditional corporate model can learn much from this approach.

Businesses considering the introduction of remote working should have a clear strategy for its implementation and understand the needs of staff and the implications upon the necessary introduction of an improved IT infrastructure.

The virtual office is almost certainly here to stay and brings huge benefits for many. But don't go headlong into working from home until you have made a realistic assessment of the pleasures and pitfalls of doing so.

Project-based Working

Another development in the changing world of work is the growth of 'project-based working'. Here's how individuals and businesses can profit from this.

The way in which we work is changing. Whereas it was once possible to have a 'job for life' this is now no longer the case. Even jobs that were once considered safe are now being turned into annual contracts with employees being asked to 'bid' each year for them. As the world continues to shrink and technology evolves, allowing people to communicate easily with far away countries, the way in which we work will never be the same.

As a result there are probably more self-employed people than ever before. But self-employment means different things to different people. One of the more recent developments is the growth of project-based working.

As employers seek to become leaner and more efficient there is a growing recognition that certain tasks can be undertaken by someone other than a permanent member of staff, particularly where the task is known to be short term. This is where the project-based worker can provide a solution.

Project-based working is not unlike freelancing. But while

the freelancer is constantly trying to sell skills to a wide variety of users, project-based working will generally mean working for just one or two employers at any time.

It can be relevant in a number of different areas:

◆ Internet services: banner design, domain registration, search engine optimisation.

◆ Marketing and creative: illustrations, brochures, logos, advertising.

◆ Web design: design, programming, e-commerce, content.

◆ Software development: business applications, technical solutions, databases.

◆ Research: market information, customer statistics, financial, trademark.

◆ Translation: interpreting, proofreading, translation.

◆ Writing: website content, speeches, technical writing, copy editing.

There are a number of websites dedicated to project based working, such as www.smarterwork.com, www.freelancers.net and www.cwjobs.co.uk.

Project-based working has many advantages, for employer and employee. Employees can take a month off work or organise work around their lives.

Once there is a profile of successfully completed projects it's then possible to market skills directly to companies who you know need help. For the employer, the advantage of having a dedicated person assigned to a specific project without the burden of full employment is equally attractive.

25

The B2B Marketplace

Sharing can change your business. Technology can give your business success in a wider market but it may mean a change from traditional trading methods – are you ready for change?

B2B – business to business – has been a buzzword in the IT industry for quite some time but the technology to enable complex supply chain solutions is only just becoming available. If the gurus are right, the advent of this new technology will change the way many firms do business.

It has been said that whilst in the past the large firm was the way forward due to high transaction costs, technology and the Internet has changed everything. Now anyone can compete on a global scale. But B2B will only benefit those businesses that are prepared to share and this will mean revising many long-held business principles.

In the world of B2B you will need to give your customers access to your IT system and work much more closely with your nearest competitors – unheard of until recently. It will no longer be good practice to concern your business solely with its part in the supply chain and operate with an island mentality. Bring customers and suppliers into the picture and into your IT system and the future will be much brighter.

Whilst these closer ties will enable you to respond more quickly than ever before to market changes they will also bring other benefits. There will be associated cost savings which will almost certainly lead to reduced prices. Your business will also benefit from a clearer view of the supply chain in which it is involved.

It would be easy to think that this is all about technology but it isn't. It's fundamentally about people – the people in your business and your customers. Survival in the new economy will be granted to those who can rid themselves of past methods and practices and who are prepared to work with their competitors in setting up virtual supply chains. This is all about customers, and they provide your profits.

The B2B market is still young and you should not rush into it without analysing your business and rethinking the way you deal with others — your company may depend on it.

26

A Question of Business

Unanswered questions about your business can affect its growth and also your prosperity. These are some of the most important areas to consider.

If you are thinking about the future of your business you probably have more questions than answers. But making sure you ask the right questions in every area of your business should lead you towards solutions that can move your business forward positively.

Expanding your business

Is your business ready to expand? If so you'll need to ensure that you plan and execute the expansion well, especially if your business is expanding quickly. Think about organisation and structure as you plan for the future.

Employment and recruitment

As your business grows you'll probably want to take on staff. So how do you go about employing the right staff for your business and what do you need to consider when employing them? Drawing up a job specification? Advertising? Interviewing? These are all easily overlooked areas.

Staff relations

Your staff are one of your greatest assets so you should treat them as such. But exactly how do you view each other? Do you have appropriate codes of conduct for all your staff, outlining steps to be taken when rules are broken?

Business communication

How do you or your employees communicate with your customers or each other? Have you lost business because of inadequate communication skills? Is there reduced production because communication is at times unclear? Are you aware of how technology could help you improve communication? If you have answered 'yes' to any of these questions, you probably need to update your business communication skills.

Good customer relations

It costs up to five times as much to go out and get a new customer as to retain an existing one. So keeping hold of these vital customers should be part of your strategy. Examining your attitude to customers can be very helpful.

Accounts and finances

How effective is your accounting system? Will it ensure the best possible cashflow through your business? Could it be better automated?

These are all serious questions, which need addressing on a regular basis if your business is to continue on a pathway to success

Finding Out What Makes Your Business Tick

Knowing the 'drivers' of your business can be vital to its success. But what do you need to monitor in order to know that you're going in the right direction?

The easy availability of modern accounting software means that many aspects of businesses can be monitored at the touch of a button. But monitoring sales, costs and working capital will only enable you to control cashflow. To give profits and cashflow a positive boost you need to focus on the real 'drivers' of your business and find out exactly what makes it tick.

If you can pinpoint the things you do in your business which are the keys to driving it forward you can often achieve a tremendous leverage and competitive advantage, enabling you to produce remarkable results with minimal amounts of extra resources.

For instance, a specialist travel agency found that low staff turnover was a driver. A quick analysis showed that an experienced sales person was three times more productive than a new recruit and that with longevity staff morale was improved and maintained. By concentrating on retaining staff the agency was able to boost sales and profitability and thereby strengthen its position in the marketplace.

For a retail business the key driver might be sales per square foot. For a manufacturer it could be machine downtime. A business providing a service might have a rapid response time to clients' requests. Returns or defect ratios, outbound sales calls, staff absence or speed of stock turn may be key.

Whatever your business there will be critical factors you can identify, track and focus your efforts on. Once you have pinpointed them, these drivers can provide the clearest possible indications as to where money, manpower and other resources can be used to greatest effect.

Knowing what makes your business tick can help you wind it up to the next level.

28

Transform Your Business

Business stuck in a rut? Struggling to stay afloat? It needn't be this way. We offer an inspirational view of how to transform your business.

Moving a business into that next stage in its development can be problematic. The following five steps may just help you to become the next Richard Branson.

Dare to dream

First you need a vision. Most great entrepreneurs have had one. Tom Watson Snr's goal was to transform his tiny company into an international corporation – it became IBM. It's easy to think 'I couldn't do that, it's just wishful thinking', and easier to get lost in the how-to of it all. The minute you start thinking like this stop and go back to the big picture – you don't need the burden of reality whilst you're dreaming.

Define the vision

Write down what your business will look like. Imagine yourself arriving there in five years time and describe what you see – the car park, the building, the people, the customers. Consider what products or services you will offer, how big it will be, what your own role in it will become.

Think outside the box

Don't restrain yourself with narrow thinking. Your initial idea and concept may be simple but try to think how you can expand it to offer other associated services or products. Wilkinson, for instance, moved from swords to razors!

Join the dots

The clearer your vision the easier it is to make it happen. Tom Watson Snr said that once he had a picture of how IBM would look and act he realised that unless they began to act like that from the beginning they would never get there. Treat challenges positively and you'll be surprised at how they can become opportunities.

Make it happen

The best entrepreneurs often write their business plans down on one sheet of A4 paper. Spilt the paper into four sections. In the first, write where you are now. In the second, where you would like to be. In the third, what needs to be done to get you there. And finally, in the fourth, who will do it all and when.

So start now and — dream on!

Author: What advice would you give to someone about to take their first employee?

Geoffrey Thompson, Managing Director, Blackpool Pleasure Beach:

'Personnel selection is vitally important, Nearly all businesses survive or fail because of people. If they don't take the selection processes very, very seriously indeed and end up with the wrong people they'll be out of business. It doesn't really matter what you do, the success of your business depends on the people you employ. You've got to ultimately make your mind up and you're either good at selecting people or you're bad at selecting people. People who are good succeed and people who are bad don't.'

Sir John Harvey-Jones:
'It's a very, very serious choice. With luck they'll be the first of many and you'll grow up together so don't get someone 'ready made', so to speak, get someone you can get on with, who is honest and pretty fearless. They'll tell you the truth and who's a grafter.'

Section 2

Managing Yourself, Managing Others

29

The Visionary Entrepreneur

The visions we have for our businesses are what makes them and us really successful. Here are some thoughts to help you realise the vision for your business.

Businesses are often started with a vision of what life will be like as an entrepreneur. What's your vision for your business? Where do you see it being in one, five, ten years? Do you have a vision for your next step? If not, how will you know what you are working towards? How will you know when you get there?

Visions, or dreams, are what your subconscious acts upon to create your reality. If you envision yourself in ten years' time as a supremely successful businessperson and you believe in the deepest part of your being that you will be successful, then your mind will subconsciously seek out ways to bring that vision to life. Equally, if you see yourself in ten years' time doing pretty much what you're doing now, then you can be confident that that's *exactly* where you will end up.

So ask yourself a few questions. Where do I want to be in ten years? What do I need to do within the next five years to bring me closer to my vision? What do I need to do within the next year to bring me closer to where I need to be in five years if I am to achieve my ten-year vision? What do I need to do within the next six months, one month, one week, today, *now*?

This, of course, is a classic goal-setting process. You've heard, over and over again, that you need to set goals in your life. To fail to set and achieve goals is to fail to achieve anything. It is only when you have a vision in mind that you can even have the starting point you need to begin to think about setting the goals that will get you there.

Setting goals and objectives in this way will help you achieve your vision. It is inevitable. Our lives are a function of our deepest beliefs about ourselves and our world. The key to success and happiness in life is to create a positive vision of what that means to you. A word of caution, though. Make sure your vision is truly what you want because you will get it. As the old saying goes, be careful what you wish for!

Entrepreneurship: Do You Have What It Takes?

Many of us would like to emulate successful entrepreneurs such as James Dyson. But have you got what it takes? Here is a list of things to consider before you take the plunge.

According to the Global Entrepreneurship Monitor 2000 only 1 British person in 25 is entrepreneurial, compared to 1 in 10 in the USA. Brazil leads with 1 person in 8 being considered an entrepreneur.

Entrepreneurship is defined as 'any attempt at new business or new venture creation, such as self-employment, a new business organisation, or the expansion of an existing business...'. It is a major contributing factor to the economic well-being of a country both in terms of economic growth and job creation.

Traditionally, entrepreneurial ability tended to focus on initiative, decision-making, innovation and risk-taking, defining the characteristics of those who chose to become entrepreneurs. Now, however, with corporate downsizing being a fact of life, many entrepreneurs find themselves thrust into the role by default.

Here's a list of character traits and work ethics common to successful entrepreneurs. Although it is not necessary that you possess all of them, you should possess most:

Passion – for the idea.
Curiosity – questioning everything.
Sponges – devouring information.
Optimism – seeing problems as opportunities.
Forward looking – never being satisfied with the status quo.
Careful about money – knowing what things cost and their value to the business.
Started earning at a young age – seeking out activities such as babysitting or lawn mowing as a teenager.
Competitive – not letting the grass grow under their feet.
Time conscious – knowing its value and making the best use of it.
Risk takers – not being afraid of taking calculated risks.
Usually loners – preferring a solitary work environment as opposed to working in teams.
Professional – always being professional in their approach to work.
High energy – having a plan and a vision, and recognising that the fitter they are, the better their minds work.
Flexible – being responsive to change.
Confident goal-setters.
Persistent – successful entrepreneurs never give up.
Learning from failures.

The allure of entrepreneurship is undeniably strong for many but make sure you're going into it for the right reasons. But if, taking everything into account, you're adamant that you have what it takes, then grab the bull by the horns and create something absolutely fabulous.

Get Creative

Creativity isn't just about design. You need to develop a culture of creativity within your business.

It's official – British business lacks creativity. It's suffering the equivalent of writer's block according to a recent CBI report, and as business people are generally so busy with day-to-day issues this is hardly surprising. But it is now well recognised that creativity is the lifeblood of all businesses, particularly if they want to grow and prosper.

However, according to author and course leader Tim Foster, most of us are 'running in neutral, doing the same things every day'. So how do you rejuvenate stale minds and attitudes to get that little extra from people, which can make the difference between doing a reasonable job and a terrific one?

♦ Have an 'open mind' philosophy and a 'can do' attitude – it's all too easy to think that our own ideas are the best and fail to encourage other members of the business to contribute. The people who actually do a job often have the best ideas for how it can be improved.

♦ Use tried and tested creativity tools and techniques. Think about holding creativity training courses –

writing, drawing, painting or acting. Hold brainstorming sessions to get answers to specific problems, but avoid using killer phrases like: 'we've tried that before', 'yes, but', 'it will never work' or 'that's a ridiculous idea!'. These are all negative, and creativity responds best to positive encouragement. Try the 'why, why' and 'how, how' techniques, asking 'Why... why' five times in answer to questions or problems – five should get you to the root cause.

- ◆ Don't be afraid to fail. If the 'can do' attitude is to pay dividends all fear of failing needs to be removed. Failure is not necessarily a bad thing. If we're succeeding at everything we're probably living on mountain tops, whereas failure tends to put us into valleys. But remember nothing grows on mountain tops.

Environments where creativity is encouraged and nurtured are a joy to work in and we all work better, more effectively and creatively when we are happy.

Management Training – Shakespeare's Way

Creativity is vital. Here are some new ways people are finding to rejuvenate themselves – and their businesses.

Not so long ago when business management teams wanted to improve their performance they dressed up in combat jackets and traipsed around a muddy field carrying machine guns filled with paint. These days, however, the arts world is keen to introduce managers to a range of other stimulation. As a result, people are writing plays, composing poetry, painting murals and playing musical instruments in an attempt to unlock their hidden potential.

Courses have been developed which can address almost any given business situation, including developing a customer base, coping with cashflow problems and learning to delegate. It may, at first, seem unlikely that a Shakespearean actor, a poet or painter would have any useful knowledge of running a business but they all pursue their artistic goals by constantly questioning everything. Take the case of the actor: actors work together in small, highly skilled teams to deliver great theatre and in creating their work need a real awareness of others in society – just as in all businesses.

The idea behind the arts and businesses working together is about unlocking those things that are hidden in all of us and raising confidence through better understanding. It's about bringing people out of their shell or 'box'. As the techniques used remove our fears and break down inhibitions we become more prepared to share ideas with others. The combination of improved confidence and self-awareness raises problem-solving abilities.

The result is improved performance, which should translate into increased profit. So if your business needs to solve a problem the answer's clear — break a leg!

$$\left(\begin{array}{c}33\end{array}\right)$$

Motivate Yourself

Getting back to work after a lengthy break, whether it's following Christmas or an annual holiday, can often be a daunting task. Here are a few tips for all those who feel a little jaded when they return.

Running a business is a difficult enough task but what do you do when that 'get up and go' deserts you? It's easy to reach the point of asking yourself why you bother, so how do you recharge your entrepreneurial batteries when they get low?

Take a moment to jot down the benefits of working the way you do. Is it for status, or money and what you think it will buy? Is it the lifestyle, being in control of your life, or the opportunities it leads to?

List these positive factors and stick them on your wall. Then when Monday dawns and you would rather stay in bed, your list will remind you why you should make the effort. Keep your goals in sight. It's hard to walk through a forest in the dark – you can't see how far there is to go or enjoy the satisfaction of seeing how far you have already come. If you work alone, identify an understanding person with whom you can talk through business issues and who will encourage you. A mentor can be helpful. Write a plan for yourself. Set tough but realistic objectives with timescales – we all react positively to these.

Use picture power or imagination to 'fix' your goals. It's easier to visualise something you can see. Savour the emotions you will feel when (*not* if) you land that order. Tell people what you are going to do – it will make you feel more committed.

Compile a record of past successes. Fill a notebook with tasks – one per page – that you wish to do. As you complete a task, reward yourself, tear out the page and keep it somewhere safe. When you feel you are achieving nothing, review your sheets to remind yourself of what you have achieved.

And finally — give yourself a pat on the back. You deserve it for having the strength of character to go out and make things happen.

34

Successful Negotiating

Good negotiating skills can mean the difference between securing an important contract and losing it. Concentrate on improving your negotiating skills and creating a win/win situation.

Everyone has some experience of negotiating, even if it's just organising the family holiday or buying a second-hand car. It's about reaching agreement on an issue between two or more parties with differing points of view. It could be anything from haggling over the price of a souvenir whilst on holiday to a complex international agreement.

Most people are afraid of negotiating, often because of the fear of losing what they already have. But negotiation is voluntary and nobody forces you into it – you can also walk away at any time. Nor does it require a tough or aggressive nature. Often, the best negotiators are understanding and conciliatory, good listeners who are willing to compromise.

The most important aspect of any negotiation is preparation. If you fail to prepare, prepare to fail. You should list the things you want to get from the negotiation – your objectives and ideal outcome, ranking these into high, medium and low priority. Then decide which objectives are fixed (i.e., not negotiable) and which are variable (i.e., you would be willing to make concessions). Decide how far you are willing to go on each issue and know your 'walk away' position.

There are potentially three possible outcomes to any negotiation but anything other than a win/win situation is always going to be ultimately unsatisfactory. It's only where both sides feel that they have got a fair deal with which they are satisfied that a win/win is achieved and future business likely.

Remember:

♦ Don't be afraid to ask for what you want but try to get the other party to make the first offer.
♦ Compromise (but never concede) and make sure that you get something in return.
♦ Trade things that are of low value to you but high value to the other party.
♦ Treat every concession as important. Listen carefully and make notes, observing people's reactions to what you say.
♦ Summarise regularly during the negotiation to ensure mutual understanding.
♦ You don't have to conclude the deal in one go; if necessary call a recess and regroup.

Your ability to negotiate successfully affects every area of your business so it's well worth improving your skills.

35

Managing Your Time to Accomplish More

How often have you got to the end of the day and felt like you'd accomplished nothing even though you'd been 'busy' all day? Time management is a skill everyone needs to learn in order to be truly effective.

Time is not elastic, it will not magically expand to accommodate all we have to do. So we have to learn to use it wisely.

We need to understand our time better. If you think of time as some formless dimension, you will fritter it away without any real consideration of its best use. And all time is not equal. If you're a morning person, that time is worth more in terms of productivity than your late afternoon time. Learn to identify your most valuable and productive time.

Reserve your most valuable time for intellectually-demanding activities. Your intermediate value time should be spent on important tasks that don't require that same level of concentration. Finally, reserve your low-value time for activities that require very little concentration.

Effectively structuring your time in terms of peak, intermediate and low-concentration blocks can make a profound impact on your productivity if you use that time intelligently. That means identifying what you have to do and, more importantly, what you *don't* have to do. A good way of doing this is to see if the activity furthers a particular objective. If it doesn't, why do it?

Estimate how much time each activity in your day is likely to take. Be realistic about what you can really accomplish. If you overload yourself you're only going to get stressed out about what you're not doing, and that makes you less effective in what you are doing. So pace yourself. Just don't waste time.

Grouping tasks will allow you to accomplish more in the same amount of time. Email is a prime example: it is far more efficient to check and respond to mail twice a day than to each message as and when it comes in.

By thinking about what you have to do and scheduling those tasks in conformity with your concentration levels as well as grouping similar activities, you will naturally make the most effective use of the time available. Your productivity will increase proportionately, and so will your bottom line.

36

Delegation

Delegating is a sure-fire way to get more out of the day. But it is something of an art.

The reason some of us find we can't quite find enough time to finish the day's work is that we often take on too many things, some of which we are not necessarily good at. To make matters worse we allow ourselves to be distracted by those around us which prevents us from achieving our set goals for the day.

The cure lies in effective delegation. But this doesn't always come easily to us and often requires a considerable act of faith. If, however, you have chosen your staff properly you should be prepared to put your faith in them.

Delegation becomes easier once you begin to establish concrete and measurable objectives with your staff. If these are made clear and specific, people will feel more comfortable about acting on their own. Nonetheless, it's important to focus on the end results and hold people accountable for them rather than for day-to-day details. Effective delegation means giving staff the tools they need to solve problems themselves. Whilst in the short term this may mean more training, it will save you time and money in the long term.

Get as much feedback as you can from monthly reports and make it clear to staff that you don't expect them to report back at every stage of a project unless you specifically ask for it. In that case let people know the critical points on which you would like them to focus.

Be specific and clear about your objectives. Offer realistic deadlines that can be achieved but be strict about meeting them. Recognise individual talents and allow people to use their full abilities to help you build your business. Most of all accept that mistakes happen. Even when the consequences are serious try to remember that some great scientific breakthroughs have come from mistakes.

If you allow people to use their abilities and learn how to take responsibility you will probably find that they do the job better than you could. In addition, you've been freed up to manage, not just firefight.

Making the Most of Temps

Hiring a temp can be the answer in a crisis. But how can you get the most out of a temporary situation?

Reaching for the telephone to hire a temp can provide a simple solution to a difficult situation. Most businesses have experienced the difficulty at least once. Either a regular staff member is ill or the workload has increased but doesn't yet warrant taking on further people.

An agency can be a more reliable source if they are experienced in matching the needs of employers and temps. This is crucial if a successful relationship – however short – is to be created. Most successful agencies say that it is essential to know both clients and temps. So it's important to deal with an agency that will come out and see you and the way you work.

When the temp arrives be prepared to spend time with them. A proper induction is advisable to make the best use of the person you are hiring. It may be useful to have a handbook detailing your office procedures and maybe even listing who's who in the business. Even showing where the coffee machine and washrooms are is important. At the very least explain fully the project they will be handling.

If the temp is a holiday replacement you may want to consider a day's overlap. This will give the temp more confidence, make them more effective and reduce the chances of other staff being put to unnecessary interruptions.

However good the temp seems take nothing for granted, especially with important procedures. Check thoroughly that they have fully understood what is expected. This should prevent someone else spending two days putting things right again.

Temps should settle in quickly, it's the nature of what they do. Where this isn't happening they should be asked to leave. Some experts say a temp needs two days, others say just a few hours. The chances are that as an employer you will have a good idea of their suitability within a very short space of time. Remember, temps are there to help you, not make things worse.

Multi-tasking Made Easy

Juggling the many different tasks required by self-employment can be difficult. Here is how to stay on the right track.

Being self-employed means you wear a lot of hats – accountant, publicity director, technical support – and spend much of your time juggling various seemingly unrelated responsibilities. Whether your speciality is marketing, translation, graphic design or computer programming, going from one task to another takes a little practice.

Organisation is the means to a smooth operation. You should have an effective record system for each client, whether it's computerised or not. This will help you when communicating with them. Remember, each client must feel like they are your only client. The key to ensuring that is constant communication, and making certain you're accessible and responsive to their needs.

If you have clients for whom you only do work occasionally, touch base with them periodically – especially when you know they have events coming up in which you may play a part. This shows your continuing interest in them, and it could also get you more work.

You must stay on track – even if your clients don't. When you're working with multiple clients that can often be a bit tricky. Careful, but flexible, scheduling is the key. Prepare a monthly agenda of each client's activities. Prioritise each by due date. Then prepare a weekly schedule – planning out specific tasks for each day. If you need input from clients in order to accomplish specific tasks, schedule yourself to remind them ahead of time, keeping in mind that your first blown deadline could be your last.

End your day by sprucing up your surroundings (do a little filing, organise your phone messages, write your to-do list for tomorrow, etc.). It will be much easier to start the next day with a clean slate.

Consistency in anything lessens the work, for both the client and you. If possible, set up all of your clients on the same billing schedule. For the most part, you should be able to prepare statements for all your clients in one day or less.

Managing multiple clients can be a challenge. But with a little preparation, some solid organisation and some genuine dedication, you'll find yourself accomplishing more than you would imagine possible.

How to Relax if You Work From Home

Learning to relax when you work from home isn't easy. It's hard to know when to take a break or keep your head down. Here are some useful tips for staying sane when you are seemingly on the go 24 hours a day in your own home.

Everyone thinks that working from home is easy – until they try it, and with the development of the 'virtual office', more and more people are doing so. Working in an real office makes life simple; yoga or yodelling can calm you down once you escape the daily grind. But how do you stay focused and relaxed when your work place is also your home?

Don't panic. When emergencies crop up in the middle of a busy day, keep a clear head and take control. Running around like a headless chicken won't help. Try to understand what's happening, and handle each problem in turn. Then put it aside and carry on.

Understand yourself. Are you making things worse? 'Awfulising' and 'rigid perfectionism' are seen as enhancing stress. Awfulisers say 'this is awful, it's the end of the world!' when it generally isn't; rigid perfectionists say 'no matter how much pressure there is on time or resources, I want to do a perfect job'. It is much better to try to do a good job.

Build relaxation into your day. Exercise cuts stress – take advantage of being able to get out at any time of the day. If you stay at your desk all day you will feel more stale and tired in the afternoon. Going for a walk and getting away from the noise of even a small office can be beneficial.

Develop healthy habits. Nicotine, caffeine and sugar may all give you a quick buzz and feel relaxing, but then you feel very flat because they are actually having the opposite effect. It may sound dull but the right diet really can help. Try water or herbal tea, pasta, rice, noodles or bread if you want to feel more relaxed.

Tense up – and let go. Curl up in your chair, draw your knees up, tighten into a ball, and then let yourself relax. You can curl up at your desk for as long as you want – one of the best things about working at home is that there's no one to see you!

Working at home can have huge benefits providing you are able to separate your work from your home life. But the chances are that at some point work will overtake home life. So don't be afraid to claim back the time. Remember, it's your life, your home and your time. You are in control.

Flipping the Switch

Turning your business off and your life on isn't always easy, especially when you work from home. So how do you 'flip the switch'?

Running a home-based business can have tremendous advantages. But learning to switch off and allow time for family or friends doesn't always come easy. Here are five ways to help you flip the switch.

Confine work to one room
If possible, confine your business activities to a certain area of the house, preferably a room that is exclusively used by you as your place of work, otherwise you will always be reminded of it.

Separate communications systems
Have separate communications systems for home and work – one telephone and fax line for home and one for work. When you are working, have your home answering machine on and vice versa.

Establish a structured routine
You don't have to be regimented, starting at 9:00 a.m., taking a one-hour lunch break and working through until 5:00 p.m. You can set whatever routine and structure you

like. The important thing is to be disciplined and not allow 'your' time to be eroded by work.

Rituals

Rituals can play a useful role in switching off at the end of the workday. For example, you may already work until your partner returns home. Perhaps you share a glass of wine together at that time. Why not think of this as an 'end of workday' ritual? In doing so, your mind will soon learn to associate it with the end of the working day.

Plan to take days off and vacations

Don't forget to schedule days off and vacations (and make sure you take them) or underestimate the rejuvenating effect of taking a complete week off.

Working from home doesn't have to mean turning your home into a place of work. By practising these simple disciplines you can be sure that even though you are taking care of business, you are also taking care of something even more important – life.

Checking References

Checking a prospective employee's references is tremendously important if you want to ensure they are the right person for the job. Here are some suggestions on how to check references effectively.

Taking on staff can be a costly business in itself and so making sure you get the best person for the job can be vital. Checking references thoroughly can help you to avoid the unnecessary costs of repeating the process. It can help to ensure that the applicant has given correct details of previous occupations and employers and has had relevant experience to the position on offer.

Methods of checking references can include:

- **Telephone:** it helps to verify the telephone number and address of any previous employer before contacting them. Try to speak with both the company manager and the candidate's direct superior if possible.

- **Written confirmation:** this will give you the smallest amount of information, but you will probably get a response from this method (include a stamped addressed reply envelope), whereas you may not from others.

- **Personal visit:** this is a time-consuming but useful method of checking references, allowing you to speak face-to-face with the applicant's previous employer, and often to gain more relevant information than with a relatively short telephone call.

- **Contracting out:** there are a number of specialist recruitment agencies that will verify references.

What can previous employers tell you?

- **Confirmation of details received:** it is useful to verify the basic details of the applicant's employment – duration, position, nature of the work and so on.

- **Reliability and punctuality:** determining punctuality, reliability and capacity for hard work are all important.

- **Reason for leaving the job:** does their version of their reason for leaving tally with that given by the employer?

- **Relationships with clients, customers and colleagues:** you will need to find out whether the applicant works well with their associates, especially if they will be working within a team.

Before contacting previous employers it's helpful to have a list of questions prepared in order to gain as much information as possible. Remember that you are probably hoping to employ a candidate for a considerable time and the more you know about them in advance the better your relationship is likely to be in the future.

Employing Part-time Workers

Employing a part-time worker can be an excellent way to help your business grow but it shouldn't be seen as an easy option requiring a lesser commitment from employers. These are some of the rights of the part-time employee.

Taking on a part-timer is no longer a casual affair as they are now well protected by regulations which provide them with a range of new rights. Part-time workers – who include agency staff and those working from home – must now be treated in the same manner and afforded the same rights as comparable full-time workers.

In practice part-timers must be offered the same basic rate of pay (including rates for overtime, sick and maternity pay), and the same entitlement to join occupational pension schemes or receive other contractual benefits such as private medical insurance or staff discounts.

The regulations are based on pro-rata principles and part-timers are entitled to the proportion of a comparable full-timer's pay and benefits according to the proportion of the full-time hours they work. Part-timers can only be treated less favourably where an employer can show appropriate justification for doing so.

Part-timers can enforce their rights at an employment tribunal, which can make a declaration of their rights and order an employer to pay compensation. They cannot be dismissed or subjected to detrimental treatment for exercising their rights.

Where a part-timer considers that they are being treated less favourably than a comparable full-time worker they can request a statement from the employer giving a full explanation of this, which should include the employer's reasoning. The employer must respond in writing within 21 days. Failure to do so, or an evasive response, will allow a tribunal to draw adverse inferences.

Most part-timers are female and it is considered that unfavourable treatment would hit them disproportionately hard. The regulations were introduced to redress these balances in the working population. It's worth remembering that compensation which can be awarded by a tribunal has no upper limit in certain cases.

Part-timers can be a considerable asset to your business, but ensuring that the conditions offered to them at the outset of their employment are in line with the regulations is essential if you're going to create a lasting, meaningful relationship.

$$\left(43 \right)$$

Managing Remote Employees

As more and more people are given the option of working at home the challenge for those running businesses is how to manage these remote workers effectively.

The teleworking revolution is very much a part of modern working as businesses of all kinds wake up to the benefits it can provide. The Internet has played a big part in this, enabling highly effective communications between managers and their staff from any geographic location. The home-working option may even play a part in helping to recruit the right staff for your business.

It does, however, bring a new set of challenges for business managers and requires the adoption of a range of new skills. Whereas in the past managers have been able to see clearly what their workforce was doing, new levels of trust are now required. But as most people respond positively to this the effects on morale, staff retention and sick leave can all bring increased productivity.

Keeping staff motivated and focused and ensuring cohesion between home workers and those permanently based in an office is vital, and it's important to keep a real sense of teamwork so that those working at home don't become resented by others. Using technology wherever possible is advisable – providing home workers with access to the company's local area network can help. Encouraging regular contact between office-based staff and teleworkers will help to combat feelings of isolation that can often arise.

It's also very important to have guidelines for the home worker to follow. You'll need to ensure, for instance, that telephone calls are answered appropriately, as maintaining a consistent image throughout your business is important. Ensure also that all telephone and Internet connection bills are paid promptly.

Working at home will seem highly attractive to many people but it also requires considerable amounts of discipline. There will be inevitable distractions and so helping staff to develop good time-management skills, providing training where required, is advisable.

As manager you will need to ensure that deadlines are met. Where a home worker seems to be falling behind early assistance to overcome the problem can prevent it becoming more acute.

Successfully handling this new type of employee can bring great rewards, achievable with effective monitoring and communication.

Handling a Freelancer

Growing your business can often be easier with a freelancer to take on those jobs you can't find the time for.

Hiring a freelancer can be a terrific way to tackle problems your staff don't have the time or the expertise to deal with, but it also presents some risks.

It is important to check out your freelancer's background, particularly if you hired them from the web, which offers lots of opportunities. Request references and samples of previous work. Some sites have implemented rating systems, which give feedback regarding the competence, efficiency and professionalism of those individuals who have already completed projects.

Clearly establish what you want accomplished. Provide samples of what you like and don't like. Be specific about what you want the finished piece of work to convey, thereby avoiding confusion along the way and disappointment in the end.

Give as many resources to your freelancer as possible with access to specific reports, generic materials such as a corporate brochure and recently-distributed press releases which can be helpful as they may contain certain terminology – or a specific tone – that is unique to your company.

Your employees should also know that it's okay to answer your freelancer's questions and provide information. Nothing will impede your expert's progress more than having to ask permission from management every time they need to ask a question or gain access to a document.

Check in with your freelancer frequently to avert problems before they get out of hand. If the project is long-term, request a twice-weekly update. For visual projects (web design, brochure layouts, logo concepts, etc.) ask your expert to post the work on the web and/or send overnight samples at specified intervals or after major revisions.

A well written contract that details job description, pay rate, payment terms, and the due date can prevent problems later on if your freelancer doesn't or can't deliver.

With a little preparation and some careful planning, you'll find that hiring a freelancer can help you to grow your business in ways you may not even have considered.

$$\left(45\right)$$

Staff Motivation

Motivating staff can increase production and profits. But how do you identify the motivational needs of the individual?

Employers and managers don't often consider why their staff turn up for work, or, more importantly, why they choose to remain in their employment. However, much more can be achieved than simply getting a job done or meeting an objective by giving serious thought to the issue of motivating your staff appropriately.

The motivational needs of individual employees will be different and over the years there have been a number of studies identifying a range of different factors, which include:

- The working environment – poor or inadequate equipment or work facilities.
- Working conditions – too hot, too cold, no breaks, long hours.
- Social interaction – isolation, socialisation discouraged, etc.
- Job security – redundancies, feeling not part of the company, etc.
- Skill or intellectual use – inability or discouragement to use intellect or skill.
- Promotional prospects and job title.

- ◆ Responsibility – not being allowed to work on their own initiative.
- ◆ Recognition and appreciation – lack of praise or recognition for achievement.
- ◆ Trust and respect.
- ◆ Participation in decision making.
- ◆ A sense of belonging.
- ◆ Salary.

You would be wrong to assume that all this simply means bowing to the pressure of the workforce in order to get them to work for you. Remember that employment is a contract between two parties requiring each to fulfil their obligations. As an employer you are trying to improve the relationship you have with your staff in recognition of the fact that the happier they are the more productive they will be, and this will impact positively on your bottom line.

How you go about investigating and satisfying your employees' motivational needs will be determined by your management style. The key to this, however, lies in the ability of individual managers and employers to identify the needs of employees without resorting to preconceived ideas.

In other words, don't assume anything about individuals, instead ask them questions. You might be surprised by the answers you receive.

Keeping Employees Happy

High levels of staff turnover can be expensive and demoralising to your business. Motivating and rewarding staff can be much more profitable.

Keeping your staff happy and satisfied and expressing how valuable they are to the business is important if you want to bring out the best in them. There are a number of different ways in which workers can be shown that their efforts and achievements are being noticed and all are aimed at improving staff motivation and job satisfaction.

- **Performance-related pay and bonuses:** earnings can be made up of rewards related to their performance and effort. Bonuses, particularly at times of the year such as Christmas and before public holidays, are an excellent way to motivate people.

- **Staff holiday incentives:** deals can often be established with travel companies to provide very reasonably-priced holidays for employees.

- **Leadership development and promotion schemes:** employees should be made aware of the realistic possibility of promotion within the company, with the option of training schemes aiming to develop their skills and realise potential.

+ **Company performance:** it is important that employees are aware of the company's performance both locally and globally and that each individual understands the part they play in the business.

+ **Share options:** many successful companies offer shares, enabling staff to be financially rewarded in the success of the business and be directly affected by its performance.

+ **Staff representatives:** it is essential that employees feel they have some control over what goes on in the office. Choose a trusted member of the workforce to act as an intermediary between staff and management – they should be able to deal with any members of staff who have concerns or criticisms.

When considering how to reward your employees, it is important to establish performance records and monitor each individual member of staff and ensure they are treated equally. It is therefore advisable to use a number of performance-based criteria – such as targets reached, punctuality, etc. – to measure achievement.

Always remember that a happy workforce is a productive one and will contribute significantly to the performance and profits of your business.

$$\left(47\right)$$

Setting and Reviewing Salary Levels

Setting and reviewing salary levels is a key business process for recruiting and retaining employees. It's important to make sure you get it right.

When making an offer of employment you should generally be paying for experience and skills rather than untested potential, while making sure that your salary levels are not substantially lower than your competitors, otherwise you risk losing key staff to them.

To get a feel for the going rate for a particular job in your industry, you should monitor advertisements in national and local newspapers, sector-specific journals, and online recruitment websites. This will give you an idea of what your competitors are offering. Alternatively, the Average Earnings Index (AEI), published by the Office of National Statistics is a useful source of information.

Pay structure

Many businesses have pay grades based on the level of skill, experience and management responsibility of the employee. Even if you don't use formal pay grades, it is still a good idea to have a written policy on salary levels so that employees can see that the criteria are consistent and non-discriminatory.

When to review salaries

Most employment contracts cause employers to review salary levels at a specified time of the year or after a certain length of service but you may also consider reviewing salaries, for example, when promoting an employee.

Conducting salary reviews

The first step is to establish how much money your business has in its budget to allocate to salary increases. Take into account turnover projections, market fluctuations and recruitment requirements.

The rate of inflation is widely used in salary bargaining but should only be used as a guide. Also consider whether you will use the same percentage increase across the board, or if increases will differ in accordance with the various grades or job functions, and decide if new recruits will be reviewed in the same way as their longer-serving colleagues.

Good practice

Many employees associate salary reviews with performance reviews. Although pay is inextricably linked to performance, it is better practice to keep salary reviews separate from the appraisal process. It is also good practice to evaluate an employee's salary separately from any benefits they receive.

Making sure your salary levels are correctly set is an important recruitment tool. So if your business is going to thrive through having the best possible staff you should make sure you get it right.

48

Managing Soured Relationships

What do you do when a business relationship goes wrong?

Frequently we hear tales of the rich and famous falling out, either with their partners or managers. These cases are of such a high profile that we almost come to take them for granted. But similar situations within the business community are more common, though less reported.

The simple fact is that some business relationships do turn sour. The important thing, however, is how these situations are responded to and how individual business people manage the situation.

Firstly, check to see whether you have a contract in place that covers as many different scenarios as possible. This should be a prerequisite in most if not all commercial relationships. Remember that a contract does not necessarily have to be in writing, though it is preferable, and it can amount to the simple signing of an official order. Where a contract is thought to be necessary at the outset of a relationship it's always better to have this drawn up, or at least looked over by a qualified solicitor.

Relationships can fall apart through misunderstanding, circumstances or intent. However, things are rarely as clean-cut as you may hope and before dashing of to the courts it's worth analysing your own part in the break-up. An ill-considered or hasty action on your part may destroy any advantage you have.

Discussion and negotiation, even where this means compromise, will always be preferable to going to court. Litigation through the courts is not for the faint-hearted and even though new procedures have been implemented in the courts system to speed things up it is always going to be a time-consuming, costly and uncertain procedure.

Early communication by all parties will generally pay dividends. And before taking any legal action it's worth considering what remedy you actually want: whether it is to have the contract completed or to receive financial compensation to cover your losses.

Above all, beware of allowing moral indignation cloud your commercial judgement and cause you to make decisions that will not benefit you. Remember, it's not personal, it's business!

Author: What does it take to succeed in business today?

Meena Pathak, Patak's Spices:
'You need to be a visionary, but also to adapt to change.'

Bill Beaumont was one of the most well-known, best loved sportsmen in the country. In rugby he rose to the highest position, captaining England to a Grand Slam. He also captained one of the BBC's Question of Sport teams where he rapidly reinforced his image as a gentle giant. But Bill is also a highly successful businessman running a textile company.

'You need strategy and you need to know which direction you're going in. Unless you have a plan you just tend to bumble on from one situation to another — as I've known to my cost in the past. I've learned from experience and by taking on professional sta, which was something I probably hadn't done in the past.'

Section Three

Presenting and Promoting Yourself and Your Business

49

Raising the Profile of Your Business

PR isn't just for the rich and famous; any business can benefit from using it creatively.

PR – public relations – can be a confusing term. But all businesses need and use PR, even if they don't realise it. Businesses have to communicate with a wide audience of customers if they are to survive. It's how well a company communicates that will determine its success levels.

The Institute of Public Relations defines PR as '...the planned and sustained effort to establish and maintain goodwill and understanding between an organisation and its publics'. In plain English, it's all about the relationship between businesses and their customers.

The majority of PR will have to be written, in one form or another – press releases, newsletters, brochures and adverts, case studies or articles. Different methods help businesses to get different messages across. But each one must be well written if it is to be effective.

Some simple guidelines that will instantly improve your business writing are:

- Keep it simple: avoid using long or technical words.

- Be as brief as possible: don't use three words where one will suffice.

- Grab the reader instantly: openings are all important. If you waffle on before putting your message across readers will switch off.

- Relate it to the readers' needs: you know your product or service is the best, but readers need to be told how it will benefit them.

- Be creative: everybody is swamped with business literature and you need to find ways to set yours apart from your competitors.

- Focus on people: people are generally more interested in other people than they are in products.

Whenever you communicate a message you are inevitably telling a story about your business. The media has an insatiable demand for stories; without them they would have very little to write about.

So remember — creative communications can enhance your business; poor communication can seriously damage it.

(50)

Ten Steps to Self-promotion

Business is highly competitive and there are hundreds of other people trying to make a living. You need to make yourself different from the others.

Step one – identify your targets. Who should you be talking to? Who are the business decision-makers in your field? The people in the purchasing department, or the managing director? Identifying the right people is crucial.

Step two – identify your unique selling proposition (USP). People will use you because you have an edge. Perhaps it's the lowest prices, or you know more about your subject. Write down ten attributes that differentiate you from your competition to establish your USP.

Step three – position yourself in your target market's mind. Your ultimate goal is for your customers to be saying 'you should try them, they are the best'. A succession of positive experiences will bring this about.

Step four – do a mailshot. If it's over six months since you did a mailing it may be time to do another. Tell the people on your mailing list some news about you and make it relevant to their needs.

Step five – ask for a reply. Some of the most successful mailings are ones which include a fax back form or a postcard. This invites people to phone or respond in some way.

Step six – create a newsletter or place an article about what you do. Try your trade magazine or local Chamber of Commerce newsletter. Use any media contacts mercilessly. Tell them about what you are doing and what's new. You can then use press articles in future sales pitches.

Step seven – do a press release. If you've got something new to say do a press release. It needs a compelling headline and introduction and perhaps an accompanying photo. Don't forget to put a contact number for further contact.

Step eight – get listed in trade directories. Newcomers and outsiders use directories as their primary reference point when they are looking for a solution to a problem.

Step nine – join a relevant club or association. Where do other business people hang out? Is there a club or other establishment where they gather? Attendance can help to smooth the way to further, more businesslike, meetings.

Step ten – be someone in the community. There are plenty of community activities that could take advantage of your services. You will then attend meetings with the local community leaders which will expand your personal network all the more.

The more you can set yourself apart from your competitors the greater your chances of being seen by your customers. Richard Branson has built an empire on being different — what are you going to do?

Business Cards

Business cards are the most common, but the most under-rated, sales tool around. Here you'll find out how to make your business card more memorable and effective.

Business cards have been around a very long time, yet they have hardly changed – and largely, they are still filed away and ignored. But they don't have to be.

Style matters. Is your card modern, crisp, easy to read, eye catching and colourful? Or is it boring, flimsy and dog-eared? Use both sides for double impact – business details on one side and your unique selling proposition on the other.

Turn your card into something people can trade in. Offer free advice or discounts if people present the card.

Business cards don't have to be flat and rectangular. You might fold yours into a mini leaflet packed with sales info and handy tips. Nor do they have to be made of card. Make them useful instead – a tile company might put their company details on a small tile and turn it into a coaster. Similarly, a car salesman might put his card inside a plastic key tag.

One home-delivery pizza company made theirs into fridge magnets. Within a day of handing these out on the local university campus, demand soared and the company recouped its outlay in a week.

People remember faces rather than names. So why not put your photo on your card? Make it in some way relevant to your business. If you sell fishing rods, have a picture of you landing that big fish.

Why stick to card? You can use computer programmes to create interactive business cards on floppy disks (but remember that not everyone will accept these from you). You can include as much information as you want, sales blurbs, photos, prices, instructions about how to use your products or testimonials from satisfied clients.

Collecting other people's business cards can generate more business than handing out your own. On average only about 10% of the people to whom you hand your cards will contact you. But you can follow up every single card you collect. So it follows that collecting cards could bring you ten times as much business as distributing them!

Remember that each card is a potential lead.

Buying Advertising

Advertising in magazines and newspapers can be expensive. Cutting those costs can make the buying decision much easier. Here are ten ways to buy advertising at a fraction of the cost.

Advertising rates in the publications you want to be seen in can appear way beyond your means. You probably also worry about whether you'll pick up enough business to justify the outlay. This is a frequent problem faced by small businesses as they try to justify the cost of advertising and assess its effectiveness.

The following plan can help you to cut those costs:

1. First, call up the advertising department and ask for the rate card. Study it carefully before ringing again to discuss your ad.

2. Remember that hardly anyone pays the full rate card price. Sales people expect you to negotiate so ask them for their best deal.

3. If you can't agree a price simply let them know they can call you any time up to publication if they have unsold space.

4. If it's not a major issue for you tell them you don't mind where the advert goes.

5. Create a reputation for yourself by paying your bills on time – bigger discounts will be offered to people they know will pay promptly.

6. Play the knife-edge game and buy late. One technique is to supply camera-ready artwork to publications with instructions to call when they have space available at 60, 70 or 80% off rate card prices.

7. Space in new publications can be bought much cheaper as the sales team will be hungry for business.

8. Avoid being talked into 'special deals' and stick to what you want as you can be sure that where you compromise your requirements you will not achieve the desired results.

9. Know when it's time to back off and save your negotiating skills for a time when the sales team may be more receptive.

10. Always have your artwork ready – you never know when the phone will ring with a really great deal on offer.

If you're in business you'll already be used to negotiating, and buying advertising space is simply that — negotiation. If you can negotiate you really can buy cheap space. And you have nothing to lose by asking.

(53)

Making a More Powerful Presentation

A powerful presentation can mean the difference between securing a contract or losing one. Always keep in mind that your customers will be inundated with competitors wanting to present their case for stealing your business.

Making presentations can be a daunting task even to the most experienced people. But it needn't be. The key is good planning and preparation, making absolutely sure that you say what you need to say and no more.

First, decide what your single key message is. Don't confuse people by trying to put over too many major points. For your presentation you'll want to focus on what you think your audience will perceive as the big issue.

Second, you want to fix your message in people's minds. So bear in mind that people remember things in three ways:

1. **Visually:** by seeing it – a picture really can tell a thousand words.
2. **Auditory:** hearing it.
3. **Kinesthetic:** feeling or doing it – often the way most people learn and accept things.

Everyone uses one sense more than another. Most of us use a combination, and this is what you should aim for in your presentation.

Third, appeal to their emotions. People buy on impulse and rationalise their purchase afterwards. So you have to find ways to get their emotional, impulsive side engaged.

Try using the following five tips to help you do this. They are the keys to making unforgettable presentations:

◆ **Start powerfully.** Make a dramatic statement – then introduce yourself.

◆ **Maximise involvement** – the more they do or respond, the more involved they feel. So ask questions, especially at the start, to get the feel of your audience.

◆ **Keep repeating the main message**, using a key phrase throughout the presentation. Remember Martin Luther King's phrase 'I have a dream...'?

◆ **Dramatise it. Tell a story.** Use colourful adjectives and metaphors. Describe a scenario – most of us have got one from previous presentations – and don't be afraid to use them in order to illustrate a point.

◆ **End powerfully.** Wrap up with a powerful conclusion, summarising the benefits and finally end with a statement that includes '...I want...'.

The way you make a presentation says a lot about you. Powerful presentations are always well prepared and well-prepared business people are usually more successful.

(54)

Successful Exhibiting

Businesses large and small show off their products and services at trade shows and exhibitions. Planning for a successful show is relatively straightforward.

A stand at a good show attracting the right prospects can be extremely effective for generating leads. However, exhibitions can be expensive in money, time and materials.

Before diving in there is a range of information that you need to find out such as who and how many are expected to attend, whether they are mostly your target prospects and decision-makers. Who are the other exhibitors? Are your competitors and other complementary businesses there? This is a very good indicator of whether or not this is the right event for you, remembering that being right next to your main competitor can be a good thing.

When the decision to attend has been made it's necessary to consider the practicalities. Who will design and build the stand? A poorly-designed, untidy, badly-managed stand implies a badly-run business. Some things, like power sockets, are expensive but worth paying for.

Consider who will man the stand when you're actually at the exhibition. Can you cope alone or do you need to hire help? Ensure that sales literature is ready on time, and that it is clearly displayed. It's not always necessary to splash out on expensive brochures as too many people just collect them; initially, cheaper, outline brochures will suffice. You can send full information packs later to visitors whom you qualify at the show. That gives you a useful reason to follow up, too.

Don't assume visitors know who you are or what you offer. Too often, people walk by a stand without getting a clue as to why they should stop and talk. So be sure that strollers can grab your main marketing messages (i.e., what you can do for them) in 10 seconds.

Pictures and graphics are generally easier to display than products. Keep graphics and lettering large, colourful, attractive and easy to read from a distance.

With careful planning, exhibitions can be invaluable marketing exercises for even the smallest businesses.

55

Event Management

Businesses large and small have to plan for conferences, seminars and training courses and need to ensure effective event management.

Whatever type of business you're in it's likely that at some time you will have to plan an event. But it would be easy to think that event management is only about organising large gatherings. However, whether the event is large or small, exciting or mundane, it has to be planned if it is to be successful.

Almost every business, regardless of its size, has to plan an event at some point in its life. It may be the initial opening of the business or of a new office, a new promotion or launching a new product, a training session or an exhibition. It could even be the monthly meeting of senior management. All of these events and many others require effective planning if they are to be successful.

Good event management is like salt in your soup – you only notice it when it isn't there! So the number one rule has to be attention to detail. A pre-event brainstorming session to make detailed lists of what needs to be done, when and by whom will pay dividends. It will also help you to identify and be clear about your objectives. Clearly identified objectives are much easier to measure against results after the event.

Additionally:

- Brief staff thoroughly on your objectives.

- Have pre-prepared forms for recording customer contact – they will be very impressed to receive your response on return to their office.

- Staff breaks are important if they are to perform at their best – give them quality time away from the event.

- Don't be tempted to leave an event early, even if it's quiet – a new customer could be just around the corner.

- Make sure you use good quality display material.

- Promote the event well with direct marketing and personal selling.

On a personal note, remember that you may well be on your feet all day, so wear a comfortable pair of shoes – breaking in a new pair at an event is not a good idea.

Planning is key to a good event. So make sure you allow plenty of time to plan, and then a bit more time to cover anything surprising that happens!

56

Networking for Success

Meeting new people can bring in extra business and consolidate your position in the marketplace to create real success in your business.

Networking is one of the best ways of getting new business. But time really is money, so you need to sort out how to use it productively, using every event as an opportunity to promote your name and your services.

Be selective about the events you go to. It's better to spend two hours once a month with a small group of people who have a specific interest in your field than attending a lot of bigger, more general events.

Most people find it difficult to talk to strangers but it's important to keep moving around and meeting as many people as possible. Quite often it will be the last person you talk to who really needs your help.

Business cards are important when you're networking. It's the only way you'll be remembered, and be contactable after the event. All contacts should be followed up quickly with a letter, phone call or email offering to help with a particular item that came up in the conversation.

Rather than simply attending network meetings try to put yourself in a key role. Offer to help with the organisation of future events or to be a speaker. You will immediately improve your status and find that people start to come to you for help and advice.

If you go to a conference be sure to contribute to the discussion. Even making a short comment will get you noticed and raise your profile, making it easier for other people to come and talk to you during coffee breaks.

You could consider hosting your own mini event with some of your clients who have mutual interests. An informal lunch with clients who have never met each other will help make new contacts and demonstrate your commitment to their business interests.

Most towns and cities have a variety of business clubs which hold networking lunches, evening meetings, breakfasts and other events where local business people get together to meet and exchange information. Joining them could add to your success. And if there isn't one, why not start your own?

57

How to Develop a Business Club to Boost Business

In business, contacts are everything. It's not what but who you know that makes the difference. So how can you spread your net wider? Here are some guidelines on how to develop your own business club.

In a survey of freelance consultants, 49% said networking with other people was their most effective marketing method. Next was word of mouth, at 13%. Networking can be amazingly powerful and, though it can be a lot of hard work to do it properly, the dividends are huge.

Obviously, it makes sense to become the centre of a big and buzzing network. Most informal networks grow organically, but one way to make networking even more effective is to formalise it by setting one up.

A network meeting or business club is an excuse to bring together people with similar aims and needs. Generally they will also have something in common in their background or work. In order to be successful it's not necessary for clubs to be large; it's quality that counts.

If you think you could benefit from networking in this way you should start by asking yourself the following questions:

- What kind of business club do you want to set up?
- What do you want it to achieve?
- Who might want to join it and why?
- Where will it meet and how often?

Organising a business club meeting works better if several of you work together. That way you can pool your contacts and ensure a better turnout. But you'll need to consider the structure of the network and how you'll run it. You'll need people – maybe committee members – to help with things like inviting speakers, handling money and stuffing envelopes.

Everything hangs on the quality of the networking and the relevance of any chosen speakers or topics of debate. One network, for instance, manages to entice high-level business people nationwide to leave their desks effectively for a day a month because it shares industry secrets with its members.

You can think of something equally inviting for your club members. And the best thing is that a good network generates its own momentum.

Communicate to Avoid Extinction

The media is hungry for business stories. But sometimes it seems that the business community doesn't blow its trumpet often enough.

'Communication' is undoubtedly one of the buzzwords of business in the new millennium. But it's also one of the areas in which many businesses fail. The simple fact is that very few customers will come to you asking what it is you do, so you have to tell them.

Ironically, most businesses have always got something to shout about. It can be anything from a new product launch to a new employee joining the team, a change of business direction or simply a move to new premises. All too often businesses miss out on good publicity simply because they are not conscious of the opportunities. Every aspect of your business will present these opportunities if you're looking for them and editors in the media are waiting to hear from you – they have lots of space to fill and are usually hungry for news stories.

Getting on the radio can be a great tactical move as part of your overall publicity effort, but you do need to have a story idea or an angle to present on a particular topic.

Selling yourself as a guest on a talk show is a great way to raise your profile and if your subject relates to a topic that is currently in the news your chances of getting on are clearly improved.

The manner in which business messages are communicated is many and varied, from word-of-mouth to a website or regular printed publication. The technological tools of today mean that it's much easier for businesses to keep in touch with customers. The success of your efforts, however, will depend on how well people are trained in the right skills and how creative and innovative they are allowed to be.

Try to respond as promptly as possible to media requests. Reporters, editors and producers are on constant deadline. If they don't get what they want from you quickly, they will not wait. They'll move on to another source. So communicate quickly or suffer the consequences.

If you get the opportunity to talk about your business in the press or media, it's important to get it right.

Mastering the Media

You can get your message across in the media, and do so effectively. Here's how.

Giving a compelling interview is never easy. But there are a few tricks of the trade that can make you sound like a real professional, make the reporter's job easier and translate into a better PR placement for you and your business.

State facts, not fiction. Proving your product is indeed the 'best' is next to impossible. So don't. Simply state the specific benefits of your product and let the consumer decide. Articulate your answers with easily understood explanations and stick to the fundamentals.

If a reporter asks: 'What's so great about your new product?' try to answer 'The great thing about our product is. . .' That's much more likely to be used because it can stand on its own without needing a 'set-up' sentence. A reporter can throw that quote in anywhere and it is a logical, understandable statement about the product.

Keep quotes and sound bites concise and articulate. If you must have a 'canned response' to a question speak conversationally, not like a robot. A good rule of thumb for answer lengths is that effective TV or radio news broadcast sound bites should be around 4–10 seconds – something you can say comfortably in about two normal breaths.

Be a well, not a fountain. Allow the interviewer to dip in and draw out your responses instead of spewing forth a tirade of unsolicited information. You will seem more genuine and less self-serving if you answer the interviewer's questions succinctly and professionally.

Speak to the interviewer, not the medium. Don't get blinded by the stage lights. Whether you are speaking to the editor of a small town, weekly newspaper or Oprah, consider the reporter as just a single person in your extensive targeted audience. Treat the interview as a one-on-one conversation. That will make you more at ease, allow you to think more clearly and give genuine responses.

If you really want to raise the profile of your business getting a grip on the media will help you. Mastering it could bring you great rewards.

Getting on the Radio

Getting on the radio can be a great tactical move as part of your overall publicity effort. We offer some easy steps to get you on air.

Pitching an appearance on a talkshow begins with much of the same groundwork as preparing for a news release or other media pitch. You need to have a story idea or an angle to present on a particular topic.

It's important for your first venture into the media to prepare a background sheet. Producers need to be assured that they are talking to a credible source. Just saying you are an expert in a particular field is not enough.

Nothing kills your chances better than approaching a talkshow with an idea that doesn't resemble the style and content of the show. If you know what type of topics the programme focuses on you can tailor your pitch, and raise the chances of an appearance.

Selling yourself as a guest on a talkshow is like any other sales call; you don't want to ring a potential prospect at their busiest time. It's much better to find out when they normally take calls. If your subject relates to a topic that is currently in the news your chances of getting on are clearly improved – so ride a news wave.

If you can demonstrate past experience in speaking engagements, lecturing, etc., the producer is more likely to take a shot a your appearance. If there's anyone who can provide a testimonial your credibility will be enhanced.

Try out your pitch with someone you know. If you can't get their interest, there is a good chance your idea will fall flat with a producer. Some experts recommend sending a pitch letter first and then following up a day or two later. This can work, but if you speak to the show's producer directly, you will be able to sell the idea at that point, as well as demonstrate your ability to engage an audience. Remember that you're selling, so the more excited you are about your project the more likely someone else will be sold on it.

Finally, go for it. Nothing ventured, nothing gained!

Author: What does it take to succeed in business today?

Edwin Booth, Booth's Supermarkets:
'Passion for your core activity. Our core activity is selling food and drink and you've got to have a passion for selling to people and for the products you're selling. It's as simple as that.'

Stuart Hayes is managing director of Leyland Trucks. He has been with the firm for thirty years and has had responsibility for just about every area of the business. He was there when the firm went into receivership, experienced a successful management buyout and eventually took part in negotiating a successful sale of the business he now manages.

'It's pretty straightforward really. I think you have to have a vision for where you want your business to be and I think that vision has got to be both optimistic and realistic. You have to have the drive to be able to take it to wherever that vision may be and you have to have capable people around you to support you in getting there.'

Section Four

Sales and Marketing

61

Successful Sales Strategies

The success of your business will ultimately depend on just how well you sell your products or services. Here are some factors which should be considered.

So, you think you've got a great product, but how do you persuade people to buy it? The more work you put into planning and developing your sales strategy, the easier it will be to close a deal and develop a loyal customer base.

Identify features and benefits. What makes your product/ service unique and how can it improve the life or work of your customer? Differentiate between a feature and a benefit and look at the product from your customer's perspective.

Check out the competition. What are others in your market doing? Evaluate their strengths and weaknesses and analyse what methods they use to sell.

Define your market. The more research you put into identifying your potential customers the more effective your sales strategy will be.

Sales methods. Once you've identified your target market and assessed the benefits your products can offer you can plan what sales method to use – personal contact (direct selling, retail), telesales, direct mail (special offers, catalogues), the Internet.

Presenting. Creating, for instance, a PowerPoint presentation including key information that can be tailored to each customer's needs can help to develop a strong, professional and consistent image.

Negotiating. Be prepared to negotiate, but know your bottom line – there's no point selling something if you lose money, even if you think it's worth it to capture a customer for the long term.

Closing the deal. You've persuaded the customer that they need or want what you have to offer. Now you have to get a firm commitment to the sale. Keep focused on your customer and capitalise on what you have learned about them during the negotiations.

Follow up. The sale is just the beginning. Following up the deal will strengthen the relationship with your new customer, and could provide opportunities for additional sales.

And finally don't forget that continually evaluating your sales process is vital if you're hoping to refine and improve it – few things are ever perfect.

You can formulate a successful sales strategy if you keep all of these in mind.

62

Inexpensive Market Research

Researching a market is critical. It is perfectly possible to find out more about the market for your business without breaking your budget.

Research can sometimes be notoriously misleading with people often saying what they think you want to hear. But just as the manager of a football team wouldn't dream of going into a game without finding out the form of the opposing side, the manager of a business should not prepare a marketing strategy without checking out the strengths and weaknesses of the competition.

Failure to understand your market is one of the most common reasons for business failure. But market research projects carried out by professionals don't come cheap. Basic research, however, need not cost a fortune and it's not rocket science.

A considerable amount of research is already available in the public domain. Good old desk research in public libraries or on the Internet (which is an increasingly invaluable research tool) can reveal information which may otherwise take forever and cost a small fortune to obtain. Alternatively, Business Link provides an extensive information service.

Your customers (and prospects) can also be an excellent way of finding out information – most of them will happily give you feedback and opinions on your products or services.

Five points to simple market research:

♦ What information is there within your business that tells something about your market – the number of enquiries for certain products, sales trends of products, salesforce reports?

♦ What published information is available on your market?

♦ What can you learn from analysing your competitors?

♦ What can you begin to do on a regular basis to ensure constant feedback from your customer base?

♦ What can you find out about your market simply by looking around?

These basic points can produce surprising results and you will not be joining the ranks of thousands of small businesses that mistakenly believe that market research is beyond them and only for the big boys. Remember, the dangers of not knowing your market could be disastrous with your business and livelihood being at risk.

Don't be afraid to dip your own toe in the waters of market research — you never know what pearls of wisdom you may come up with.

63

Writing Effective Sales Letters

Writing a good introductory sales letter is often what gets you in to see a prospective customer.

Writing letters is something we all do, often without a second thought. It's something we easily take for granted. As a result, sales letters are frequently dispatched in less than perfect form and fail to produce the desired result.

The real purpose of a sales letter is often overlooked. Most sales letters, for instance, are intended as 'door openers' rather than actual sales documents – seeking to begin a dialogue rather than make an immediate sale. It's important, therefore, to define your aim precisely before writing the letter.

Content
♦ **Keep it simple and brief:** avoid using long or technical words and don't use three words where one will suffice. Keep the length to a minimum – readers don't want to read two pages of waffle which could have been summed up in less than a page.

♦ **Openings are vital:** get the readers' attention immediately, otherwise they will switch off.

◆ **Relate to readers' needs:** clearly show the benefits the reader could gain.

◆ **Split the content up:** use bullet points and highlighted headings to add clarity to the letter.

What to send

Whilst people are generally more willing to open direct mail these days, it soon goes into the bin if they don't like what they see. Research suggests that around 70% will not read something that looks cluttered. So give consideration to the look of what you are sending. It is worth asking people who fit the profile of your target about what impresses them in a mailing or sales letter.

Rewriting

Even the best writers expect to rewrite something in order to get it right. It may seem like wasted time, but try to think of it in terms of increased sales. That extra five minutes spent rewriting a letter may bring in the best contract you've ever had. If you need more guidance, go through the 'seven steps' that follow.

Your sales letters can impress a target or quickly turn them off, so it's important to get them right.

Seven Steps to Successful Sales Letters

Here is more advice on the task of writing sales letters; it's not as difficult as you might think. And the help you find here doesn't only apply to sales letters; it can apply equally to brochures, general sales literature and even web pages.

1. Grab attention with an eye-catching headline.

This might be a question or statement that will ring a bell with all your prospects in one go. Keep it quite general to identify with as many people as possible.

2. Provide a reason to read on

Headlines hook prospects and lead them to your next line. There you start to build interest and ensure they read the next sentence... and each subsequent one.

3. Explain why the product or service is relevant

It helps to look at things from the reader's point of view. Relate the product to the customer's agenda in terms of its benefits. Show them that it will make their life better, safer or easier. How will it save them time or money? Look at their ultimate goal and relate it to that.

4. Why you?

Briefly explain why they should buy from you. Give them comfort reasons and confidence, showing what makes you the expert. Add credibility. Use testimonials from happy customers.

5. The offer and call to action

Once you have nailed down the key benefit and positioned yourself as the person to deliver it, make an offer.

6. Make it easy and worthwhile to respond immediately

Link the offer to a desired action and a deadline. For example 'Ring before [date] for an appointment to discuss this, and I will send you a free booklet...' Relate the incentive to your product, or make it universally appealing.

7. Prove there's nothing to lose

A common fear about a remote sale is that the product will not live up to expectations. This fear can make people hesitate for so long that they never respond, no matter how attractive the benefits and your offer. You can overcome this by offering a guarantee or refund.

Remember, if you go about writing sales letters in the right way, and are clear about your aim from the start, you should always be able to hit the target.

How to Make a Sale

You don't have to be a born salesman to get orders. You don't even have to enjoy selling. You just have to be clear about what you want and what you have to offer. Here are ten top tips for improved selling.

1. Research your market carefully. Don't waste time trying to sell to people who don't need your product or who have no power to place an order.

2. Get past the receptionist and on to the decision-maker. Be cheerful and polite, have – and show – a good knowledge of the target company. Explain that what you offer will need to be assessed by an appropriate manager.

3. Where possible make appointments. Different businesses will have different 'best times' to see them. You'll struggle to catch a builder or farmer when the weather is good and remember that most people still adopt the traditional lunchtime.

4. When arranging appointments always offer a choice. Asking 'Which is better for you?' makes them choose, and is better than an open-ended 'When would be good for you?' which can elicit a negative response.

5. If you're selling a product that needs demonstrating make absolutely certain that it's working perfectly before you leave for the appointment.

6. Know exactly what you want, but try to think, talk and respond from the buyer's point of view. Sell the benefits and not the features of your products or service. Remember that the likes of Kodak don't sell films, they sell memories.

7. Try to ask, early on in the conversation, questions which cannot be answered with simple 'yes' or 'no' responses. Open questions lead to improved discussion, and if you're listening closely to the answers you should be able to work out any problems the buyer may have. You need to know these if you are going to sell solutions.

8. Take objections seriously, but try to turn them to your advantage. Think creatively about how you can offer to overcome objections and make sure you fully understand each objection before addressing it.

9. Recognise buying signals – questions like 'Will it take unleaded?' and 'What guarantees do you give?' When you begin to hear these close the sale quickly.

10. Never forget to go for the close and don't be embarrassed about asking for the order – that is what you're there for, after all.

Be clear about what you're trying to achieve, plan your sales efforts properly and soon you'll be selling ice to Eskimos.

Cold Calling

If you are in business, telephone selling is something you have to do – even though you may not like it. Here are some useful pieces of advice on making it easier.

Picking up the telephone and making a cold call is one of the easiest ways of getting business, yet lots of us are terrified of doing it. It's also too easy to put off making cold calls until you've done something else – had a cup of coffee or opened the mail. But the process can be made a whole lot easier if you simply prepare in advance.

Cold calling can also be an exhausting process and you will be much more effective if you run a co-ordinated campaign which you organise and record carefully. Making a number of calls in batches is often a good way to begin. So is setting objectives, such as exactly when you will ring, how many calls you will make and your targets. Remember that cold calling is a numbers game and so whilst targets are important they need also to be realistic.

Avoid being vague or over-general with your sales pitch. And whilst it is tempting to try to get business by offering an 'I can do anything' approach, success often comes when focus is narrowed down to your strongest areas. This can also have a secondary effect in helping switchboards identify exactly who you should speak to – which can often be vital.

Scan local newspapers and *Yellow Pages* for target companies and make lists of who you should ring and work out a good script or pitch. Remember that you probably have less than 30 seconds to hook people, so you need to think of really good opening lines, something they will remember. Detailed notes of all calls and responses are imperative if you want to be organised and effective.

If you really can't face the task of picking up the phone you can always try one of the growing number of telemarketing agencies who, for a generally modest sum, will make your appointments for you.

If you need more support, go through the points in the next piece – 'sales calls'.

Telephone selling can be a powerful and cost-effective tool and practice is often the way to success. Don't dread it; think of the benefits it can bring. Remember that the next call you make might be the one that secures your future.

Sales Calls

Every business needs sales in order to thrive – and telephoning can help to generate those sales.

Selling on the phone need not be as difficult as we sometimes think. The key to making a successful sales call is to remember a few points – classic selling techniques – and have a specific objective in mind, without which you risk spending a lot of time on 'courtesy calls' that never reach the selling stage. It's nothing to be nervous about.

Identifying the real decision-maker – the person who will confirm or decline your order – is the first step. You may have to start further down the chain and work up through it, but you should always know who the real target is and who you'll have to win over in the end in order to make a sale.

When you begin the process:

- Always remember to ask open questions that further the conversation and don't invite simplistic responses.

- Explain your product or service in terms of the client's needs and requirements, clearly pointing out the benefits it offers.

- Try to remember that objections don't necessarily mean a definite no, but are often a sign that the customer is interested in what you have to offer. Deal with them without hostility or irritation and then try to close the deal. If you are unsuccessful, start the selling process again.

- You may want to use a special situation to close a deal – the product might be in short supply or on special offer for a limited period of time.

- Always try to ensure that you, and any sales people you have, see things from the customer's point of view and review your sales strategies to see how they can be improved.

Successful selling is about technique, but it's also about people. Whenever you begin a sales pitch to someone try to keep in mind that you want this person to buy your products for the next twenty years and more. What you're entering into is therefore a relationship, and few long-standing alliances are based on poor relationships.

(68)

Increased Results from Customer-focused Sales

Consumers increasingly want goods and services tailored to meet their individual specifications.

In today's marketplace it's a question of 'this is what I want, now who's going to give it to me?' According to the Henley Centre, this has resulted in a complete shift in the balance of power. Consumers now have so many options that they know they can get exactly what they want from somewhere.

The successful companies of the future will be those who are totally customer focused and value the relationship they have with customers. At present 68% of customers who fail to continue doing business with a company do so because they feel that the company can't be bothered with them.

A recent US News and World Report showed why customers are lost:

- 1% die
- 3% move
- 5% develop other relationships

- 9% go for competitive reasons
- 14% leave because of product dissatisfaction
- 68% go as a result of an indifferent attitude shown towards them.

This shows clearly the need to have effective customer relationship management in place.

Accountancy firm KPMG conducted interviews with business leaders to help the Marketing Council find out how companies focused more effectively on customers. Amongst many findings winning customer preference was at the top of the list. But how is this achieved?

David Freemantle, the author of a book called *What Customers Like About You,* says that whilst many companies have tried to improve their customer service few have actually succeeded. His research suggests that where companies consistently deliver excellent customer service (and get the resultant sales) all the staff added some sort of emotional value to the customers' purchasing experience. Successful firms have staff who live and breathe their brand and rather than working from a conventional 'unique selling proposition', they connect with customers through a 'unique emotional proposition'.

The key is in creating a total experience that customers value because it makes them feel special, and in making sure the whole company is designed for customers. Then you can concentrate on forming lasting customer relationships.

Lasting Customer Relationships

Always remember that profitable business starts and ends with the customer. Being customer focused and placing them at the centre of all your thinking creates an environment that fosters long-term success and lasting relationships. Here are 10 things you can do to help this process.

1. Set yourself apart from the competition: give your customers something they can't get elsewhere. Make your niche something of real value and people will come back again and again.

2. Don't waste time on activities that can be automated: embrace new technology and allow it to free up your time so you can concentrate on the important stuff – your customer.

3. Eliminate the time you spend on non-productive tasks: handle paperwork on time and then file it instead of stacking it in a pile. All these little things add up to lots of wasted time that could be spent on your customer. For instance, unsubscribe to email newsletters you never read instead of deleting them each time.

4. Concentrate your efforts on marketing to the people that need your service: start by auditing your marketing and sales data to find out how and why a sale is made. Eliminate or change marketing strategies and services that don't serve the needs of your customers.

5. Respond to email and messages quickly: response time for email should be under 24 hours. By responding quickly you send the message that your customers are important and you are genuinely interested in meeting their needs.

6. Follow up on sales orders: make sure your customer is thoroughly satisfied with their purchase and offer them additional services related to it.

7. Give refunds promptly and unconditionally.

8. Ask your customers to fill out a survey so you can better understand their needs: offer a valuable freebie or a discounted service for participating. This strategy establishes a dialogue between you and the customer and helps determine the direction of your business.

9. Publish a newsletter: give your customers valuable tips and information they can't get anywhere else.

10. Make your website easy to navigate: customers value their time and appreciate finding what they want quickly and effortlessly.

Never forget that most of your new business will come from existing customers, so it's worth giving them the attention they deserve.

70

Marketing on a Shoestring

Even the smallest marketing budget can have a useful impact on your business. But you need to focus your efforts and make sure that every pound counts. You need to think clearly and draw up a realistic strategy.

Whatever the size of your business the chances are that you want to see it grow. That is, after all, why most people go into business in the first place, and even the tiniest amount spend on marketing can carry you a long way. So, having decided that you want to give your business a boost with a co-ordinated marketing strategy, where do you start? The number of publications is huge, so how do you choose between them and how do you turn those often generalised theories into effective business practice?

Fortunately, the first principle of marketing is just the same for a business on a small budget as it is for a well-heeled multinational: know your market. To market effectively, you need first to know who your customers are. Neglecting this most basic requirement is the most common reason for a failing market strategy.

Basic marketing is not complicated and your chief, and cheapest, marketing resource is a clear head and a systematic approach. Once you have identified exactly who, and where your customers are you can plan the most effective ways of reaching them and hopefully cut out your competitors in the process.

The routes you can choose from are many and varied – mailshots, advertising, telemarketing, energetic PR campaigns aimed at trade and local press, handouts and leaflet drops, exhibitions, launching a simple website or even putting cards in shop windows in particular areas.

Marketing considerations affect the full range of business practice, from market research to pricing, promotion to distribution, selling to customer care and more.

Even the smallest business can benefit from thinking strategically and, once written, your marketing plan should be the basis for all your business activity.

71

How to Market Your Business Globally

The lure of foreign markets can be appealing for businesses seeking to expand. This will lead you through some of the pitfalls which await the unwary entrepreneur.

Marketing is difficult enough at home, but in international markets it's much more complex. You may need to account for diverse cultures, economies, and laws. This will involve an analysis of the financial risk, economic situation, import regulations (such as tariffs, quotas and restrictions) and other factors that could affect successful market entry.

There is no guarantee that your product or service will be acceptable in another country without some modifications – from packaging to translation of text into another language. It would be foolish to assume that language barriers can be overcome by simply translating your advertising material into the home language.

There may also be legal, social, cultural and other barriers to overcome. Equally, images of men and women that are acceptable across Europe could be seen as deeply offensive in many Middle Eastern countries. And pay attention to brand names – something that sounds completely innocent in English might be offensive or ridiculous in another language.

Having decided that you want to enter an overseas market, there are a number of options available for getting your product or service to the customer.

1. Set up your own manufacturing facility in the host country. This is the most expensive and riskiest but some of this can be offset by looking at alternatives such as licensing, franchising or contract manufacture.

2. Manufacture the product at home and use overseas agents or distributors to sell it into local markets. Distribution rights are usually granted exclusively to one company. However, the task of finding suitable overseas agents and distributors for specific products can be difficult.

3. For smaller businesses, a more manageable short-term strategy is to use export houses. These offer the advantage of being based in your home country and therefore, easier to locate, and administration and logistics are reduced to a minimum.

Finally, it is worth noting that companies who have a presence on the Internet will automatically have access to international markets.

If the product you are supplying can be delivered by post, or if you are providing an 'online' service, the problems normally associated with international marketing can be avoided, or at least minimised.

(72)

Broaden Your Horizons With International Sales

The business world is shrinking as far away countries come seemingly ever closer. And with the advanced communications tools available to all businesses the ability to sell products and compete on the international stage has never been easier.

But whilst many companies have the potential to grow through exporting into new markets they are reluctant to do so for a variety of often well founded reasons. Exporting can indeed be fraught with complexity, pitfalls and risk, particularly if the necessary skills are not available.

However, it is possible for exporting to be made much simpler:

◆ Research is vital: even experienced exporters should carry out regular market appraisals, but research is not a substitute for decision. The results may be inconclusive and you'll have to decide whether or not take the risk.

◆ Evaluate the costs thoroughly: research costs money but the real costs start when, for instance, products and packaging have to be changed to meet customer specifications or a distributor needs continuous marketing support.

- Concentrate on a just a few markets: select those with sufficient potential where your product has competitive advantage – small markets may have niche opportunities and less competition; visit the market yourself.

- Talk to leading buyers and visit as many exhibitions as possible.

Real opportunities exist in areas such as the Asia-Pacific region where the world share of imports has doubled over the past twenty years. The area is built on a strong economy and financial wealth and offers exporters one of the best prospects for sustained highly profitable growth anywhere in the world.

Business Link can offer advice to help businesses develop their export potential using the specialist service of Trade Partners UK. This can offer an opportunity to become involved in a full programme of international trade activities from trade missions and export sales training to joint ventures and partnerships.

What are you waiting for? The world's your oyster.

Expanding Abroad

Breaking into foreign markets can provide additional growth and profit. Here are some alternatives for those businesses seeking to broaden their horizons and tap into new potential.

Directly exporting your goods into an international market is only one way of expanding abroad. Other options include licensing, joint ventures and offshore production.

Licensing requires a contract between you and a foreign company, which grants them the rights to manufacture, distribute and sell your product, in return for which you receive payment. It's a method that enables rapid entry into a new foreign market without making huge investments but which can provide comparatively quick returns. However, you will lose control over manufacturing and marketing of the goods: if you're not careful your partner can become your competitor.

Joint ventures, however, create what can be a more equal partnership, based on a contractual arrangement with a foreign partner. The contract can provide for different levels of equity to suit individual requirements. In some countries, a joint venture is the only legal way for a foreign company to set up operations. It has the advantage of providing a level of control over the operations, which is supported by the foreign partner's knowledge of the market. Often the partner's business and political contacts may help to smooth out difficulties. However, it will need higher levels of investment than licensing and requires training, management and transfer of technology. You will also be dealing with entirely new management in a different country on a more regular basis; where the partners do not share the same language this can create communication difficulties.

If greater overall control is your desired aim then you may consider setting up your own international manufacturing base. In doing so you may achieve lower production and transportation costs and other tax or foreign government investment incentives but the risks are relatively high. You will need much higher levels of investment than required for either a joint venture or licensing operation. Additionally, substantial time commitment will be needed. This route to market raises many issues you will need to consider such as legal and tax ramifications, and location.

These are complex processes and you may wish to take advice from an international trade adviser who can provide invaluable help, but they should certainly be considered.

Insuring Your Deliveries

Making sure your products are insured whilst in transit is vital if you want to avoid loss.

Ensuring adequate cover against damage or loss of goods in transit has saved many firms considerable sums of money and possible damage to their business. Put simply, the products you supply to your customers are, more often than not, your responsibility until the customer takes delivery.

A goods-in-transit policy can protect you from theft, loss or damage caused by accidents during transit and in some cases the consequences of any resulting delay. As with other forms of insurance, you will need to agree on the value of the goods. If the goods are new then this shouldn't be too much of a problem.

You should check the type of cover being offered. New for old is obviously the better option but it can be expensive and you must ensure that you value the goods at their replacement rather than actual value.

Some policies will offer special features such as legal expenses, cover for possessions in your vehicle, food spoilage in freezers, garage cover, outbuildings cover – but if you want to keep premiums to a minimum these can be left off. You could also offer to increase the amount of excess on the policy, as this will often reduce the premium paid.

As with all insurance the level of risk will be the determining factor in the amount of premium you are asked to pay. Remember that it's important that you give full disclosure of all facts and circumstances which might affect the policy, as failure to do so could invalidate it at a later date. If, for instance your company has a record of regularly losing goods, then you are likely to find the premiums more costly.

In order to get the best possible quotes work out the value of the goods before shopping around and examine any limitations and upper limit payouts before accepting the insurance.

Remember that insurance policies are legal documents so you must always read the small print in them — you might be surprised at what you find. You don't want to discover loopholes later.

Author: What does it take to succeed in business?

Dawn Gibbins was aptly dubbed by *The Sunday Times* as the 'bubbly boss' of flooring firm Flowcrete. She is indeed bubbly and was also named as the Veuve Clicquot Business Woman of the Year (02/03). Having grown her £25M business from nothing Flowcrete is now the world's No 2 manufacturer of specialist industrial and commercial flooring.

'Lots of energy and enthusiasm and a great will to succeed. To succeed you've got to have a vision of where you're going and you've got to persuade people to follow you.'

Stelios Haji-iannou:
'In my case £5 million from my father and a lot of luck but I realise that this may not be an option for everyone. And anyway, I suppose I did have more than that. I had a classic business education so before the Easy Group goes into any new business we make sure we study it carefully....And finally, at the risk of stating the obvious you need to be prepared to work hard.'

Section Five

The Internet and its Implications

75

Do I Need a Website?

Most businesses think they should have a website – but what sort of site should you have?

One of the first things people think they need as soon as they set up in business is a website. But first you should decide whether it's really a necessity and worth the financial investment, as not all businesses will need a presence on the Internet.

Once you have decided that a website will enhance your business there are a few points you should consider. Every week there is something new on the web, making it almost impossible to keep up. Restrain yourself from jumping on the bandwagon and looking for all those little novelties that you think make websites more interesting – the chances are you don't need them yet.

The more bells and whistles there are on your site the more difficulty users are going to have in viewing it. That doesn't mean you have to avoid new concepts in technology, but be aware that not everyone will be able to enjoy the benefits of these features. Avoid excessive graphics and frames, lots of background images and other graphic tricks as these will bog down your site and make it difficult to navigate.

The most important thing about a website is that it is simple and easy to access. Try to get to the point of what you are saying on the first page, or at least give people some idea of what your site is about. If people have to go hunting they may just decide to move on.

Split your information into logical sections and make sure your starting page is attractive and well laid out. Keep a consistent theme throughout the site and use colours, styles and fonts that complement each other.

Ask yourself what people will be looking for and try to make those things accessible from the main page. Offer a way of searching your site and make sure visitors don't have to wade through endless links to find what they want.

Remember, if your website is worth having, then it's worth thinking about clearly — the end result will reflect your business.

76

Real Methods for a Virtual Approach

We all know we've got to use the Internet; it's been compared with electricity, the telephone and car as the most significant contributor to the way we do business. But it can be confusing.

It's easy to get online but whether there is any real benefit to your business is another matter. What, for instance, would a website do for your customers – how would they benefit from it? The answer for some businesses is negative, and they need to beware of Internet hysteria.

For many the Internet is a must, but whilst it may seem like a fabulous new toy fundamental business principles must still be applied. A website alone is not going to transform your business or sales. You may even ruin other marketing efforts by over-promoting your website.

One business sent out a mailshot split in three ways:

1. Not mentioning the website – generated 170 paid orders.

2. Identical, but web address mentioned – generated 110 orders.

3. Invited people to save 25% of their time and order through the website – 2200 visits but only 7 orders.

The web address distracted people from ordering immediately. This shows the importance of websites being an integral part of the business plan and an addition to the marketing mix, but one underpinned with traditional marketing methods.

Websites are often treated as just another company brochure, which risks missing out on the chance of improving the way business is done. Being just a click away from your competitors, the Internet creates the opportunity to innovate and gain increased competitor advantage.

Promoting your website is vital, but traditional methods of doing this should not be ignored. Dot.coms have used traditional marketing methods to promote sites. Do this as often as possible but always remember to give people a reason for visiting.

Above all else remember that businesses deal with people and e-commerce is not about interacting *with* computers but *through* them. The Internet offers the opportunity to make interaction with customers much more effective.

E-commerce

The e-commerce revolution is well on its way. Here is how to ensure that success will come from a website.

The Internet revolution has begun and many firms are being swept along in its wake. Yet many businesses still don't understand how they can benefit from a website and a presence on the World Wide Web.

Most people who use the net on a regular basis will probably say that it has dramatically changed the way they work, and it is having a similar effect on the business world. This means that it has to be treated seriously and given the same respect and levels of investment as any other important corporate tool or machinery.

Businesses wishing to adopt a successful approach to e-commerce will embrace it with flair, creativity and customer focus. But in order to achieve this it is necessary to invest in thorough staff training in Internet-related applications. If staff are unprepared and lack the necessary skills to carry out e-business procedures the strategy of the whole business will collapse.

Business to business e-commerce is actually growing at a much greater pace than the business to consumer sector and this is likely to continue for some time as more and more businesses switch on to its benefits. Businesses need to be aware that once their website goes live it is there for the whole world to see. The size of the business is irrelevant. Speed is often what counts in the new economy. This can mean speed to market but is more likely to mean speed of response to enquiry and fulfilment of orders.

Businesses can grow very quickly using the Internet as their shop window but not all companies will benefit from it. Merely having a website will not guarantee success as this must be backed up with systems, be they manual or technical, which can cope with the demands which will be placed on them by individual expectations of the Internet.

But even when a good website is well supported the one thing that will continue to provide success for businesses is a sound strategy. Without this even the best-looking sites, and the businesses behind them, will fail.

Growing an Online Business

If you do want to do business online you need to do the right things at the right time.

There are many things you should be doing to market your online business. You don't have to do every one of these activities every day but if you aim to do at least a few your e-business will benefit.

Search engines and directories. Firstly, submit your site to as many search engines as possible. The main ones are **www.yahoo.com**, **www.altavista.com**, **www.google.com** and **www.hotbot.lycos.com**. It can take time to get listed so start early. You can visit **www.searchenginewatch.com** for the latest news on search engines and what you can do to improve your ratings. Visit **www.jimworld.com** for links to directories.

Publish an e-zine. This is simply an online magazine. Write your own original articles rather than relying on others. Include a reminder to visitors to recommend you, asking them to forward it to their friends and family.

Negotiate reciprocal links. Find websites that target the same people as your site and arrange reciprocal links – this simply means that each of you links to the other's site. **Identify commonly searched-for keywords.** This allows you to create doorway pages to submit to the search engines – a simple page targeting a particular keyword.

Monitor your search engine rankings. Don't become obsessed, as search engines are only one source of traffic. You will find a lot of traffic comes from other sources.

Negotiate joint ventures and co-ops. Find people to do joint ventures with – whether it is for e-zine subscribers or selling your products together as a bundled package. There is no limit on the types of joint ventures and co-operatives you can negotiate.

Offline promotion. Don't forget to promote your online business offline – in magazines, newspapers or any other form of advertising.

Host a forum. Host a forum at your site and contribute to other forum discussions. This will keep visitors coming back for more. Contribute to those run by others to establish yourself as an expert in your field.

All these represent a lot of work and a serious investment of time. Once you have an established online presence, though, they also represent a good range of activities that will help grow your online business.

79

E-laws in Cyberspace

Online trading is growing and so making sure your business is operating legally and complying with current requirements is vital.

Business today is complex. In addition to coping with the day-to-day issues that have always been present we now have the exciting prospect of doing business virtually across the Internet. But as with all forms of new transaction there comes new legislation.

As the Internet continues to grow across the world and more and more business is conducted on it the number of legal actions, particularly in the US market, is also growing. This is bringing new laws across Europe with specific directives to protect consumers' rights.

Generally, these directives that relate to online trading affect data protection and distance selling, the latter specifically giving consumers a 14-day cooling off period within which they can cancel a contract without liability. For more information on data protection, read the article in Section Six. As well as this perhaps the most important areas to be aware of are:

♦ The electronic exchange of data (EDI) is now governed by legislation. This can be of particular importance where computers automatically replenish stock or if payments are made using Internet banking systems.

◆ Contracts entered into online must still comply with contract law and contain elements of offer, acceptance and consideration. You should also give thought to the aspect of digital signatures, probably always having these supported by written documentation.

◆ Copyright and intellectual property rights apply in the same way as they do elsewhere. In cyber terms, however, they can apply to business models, website designs, navigation tools, ordering systems and domain names. You can't, therefore, copy another website and add your own name and products. Remember also that you can only transfer your intellectual property rights by an actual written agreement.

◆ If you've got Internet partners you may well need confidentiality agreements to cover the discussion of sensitive information.

◆ Certain aspects of marketing are also covered. The use of keywords (meta tags) used for attracting search engines is now controlled.

Cyberspace brings together worldwide cultures requiring common laws to control it. Your business is no longer just an enterprise, it's become the Starship Enterprise and you're now the Captain...

80

How to Begin a Web Article

Writing for your website requires a different approach to most other forms of writing. Here's how to make sure readers carry on reading.

'Begin at the beginning, and go on till you come to the end: then stop.' Web readers would be eternally grateful if web writers always followed that piece of advice.

But all too often writers do nothing of the kind. Instead of beginning an article about growing tomatoes with a clear statement about what you can expect to read they will either begin with an anecdote or, perhaps most common on the web, superfluous personal information: 'My name is John, I've been an amateur gardener for three years, and I created this page...'

Such indirect openings for articles are fine for certain kinds of writing. But in most web writing – especially business writing – the best way to begin is with the shortest and clearest statement you can make about your topic.

People are usually looking for information on the web, and if you make it easy to find they will thank you. If you make it hard to find by burying your introduction in the second or third paragraph, no one may read your article at all. Research shows that web readers scan pages before they read anything and they may scan right past your article if it doesn't have a straightforward intro that includes key words about your topic.

Writers often opt for indirect leads because they are insecure. They fear that what they have to say will be so unexciting that potential readers will be turned off, so they try to find an indirect but more interesting way to draw the reader in. But doing this actually makes things worse. If you're writing about tomatoes, and the reader isn't interested in tomatoes, it's better to get it over with fast. Readers who have had to wade through several paragraphs before finding out they're in the wrong place will be all the more annoyed.

So be courageous when you sit down to write, and don't blame yourself if it takes a while to come up with an opening that works. As anyone who has tried to write knows, beginning is often the most difficult part of the writing process.

81

Bad Web 'Righting'

As businesses rush onto the web many are forgetting that the way the site content is written is as important as the design.

Bad writing is the rule rather than the exception on the web. One reason for this is simply that good writing is hard to do, but another is that many of the people who have been involved with the web from the beginning have been slow to realise that writing is a very big part of the online experience.

If you read much on the web, you probably encounter such simple 'righting' errors all the time. The 'righting' for 'writing' mistake is one your word processor's spell-checking function can't recognise ('righting', of course, is a perfectly good word, as in 'righting a wrong'). Chances are that your grammar checker, if you use one, won't catch it either.

You'll also encounter a lot of content that's poorly organised, poorly reasoned, poorly presented, or just plain poorly written. Since writing wasn't originally perceived as a central activity in creating a website, many companies and organisations that put out large quantities of content – organisations that are, in effect, publishers – have never bothered to create the kind of editorial infrastructure that a publisher must have.

Learning to write is like learning most other things – you learn by doing, and so you learn to write by actually writing. Writing for the web requires the same expertise as any other writing, only more so. Readers on the web, for instance, apparently have a much shorter concentration span and information has to be presented in a much punchier style, using shorter sentences, paragraphs and more bullet-pointed text than normal.

If you want to write and produce your own website content it's worth going along to a writing course where you can learn to brush up your skills.

The number of websites that are badly written and badly edited remains vast, but if you look at the successful, high-volume websites, you see professional editing. The headlines are snappy and the writing is tight, for instance, at news sites such as www.cnet.com and www.cnn.com.

Well written content will bring people back to your site time after time. It's a vital ingredient of any website.

82

Email Lists

The creative use of email can enhance your reputation and that of your business. Used effectively, email can promote news and discussion.

The chances are, that if you're online, you already subscribe to an email list. For the purposes of staying in touch, whether it's with customers or colleagues, lists often do a better job than actual websites. At the same time they provide an effective way of directing customers and clients to the further resources available at a site.

Simple in concept and as useful as anything on the Internet, email lists were once a hassle to set up and manage. Now, with do-it-yourself list sites, anyone can run a discussion list or an email newsletter for free, whether you're a design expert looking to update clients on your latest projects, a retailer or a manufacturer aiming to announce product releases.

Businesses large and small use email lists in creative ways to stay in touch with customers. Email lists and newsletters have the special advantage of being 'viral'; if you provide information that's useful, your customers may pass it on to friends and colleagues, thereby spreading the word about your business.

Retailers often have a weekly newsletter updating customers on specials, sometimes offered only to newsletter subscribers. This provides an incentive for customers to subscribe, along with a way to highlight specific products.

Specific work areas often have email lists for discussion of industry issues. This is not a method of outright promotion, but being the moderator of a respected industry list is one way to raise your profile within a field, whether you're a freelance writer or a graphic artist.

Consultants, freelancers and others sometimes use email newsletters to provide information of interest to their clients and customers. An illustrator, for instance, might update clients on current work, a programmer about new ways to optimise their systems.

If you're thinking about developing your own list a number of companies now offer free, web-based software for managing email lists. You should also look at other lists to see what tactics they use to gain and retain your attention.

Email lists can be a great way to keep in touch with what's going on in your area of expertise or even find out about potential new work. Join one — you may be surprised at what you find out.

83

Writing Emails That Work

The impact of the Internet is clearly huge and email communications already play a big part in the way business is done. How do you write more effective emails?

The language of the Internet is indeed different and writing emails is becoming increasingly important. Ten billion emails are sent every day and it would be easy to think that the Internet is changing the English language beyond recognition. That doesn't need to be the case.

Keeping your messages tight and bright is vital if you want your readers to stay with you, and writing techniques you have used offline need to be applied even more strictly online. For instance:

◆ Headlines must sing loudly.

◆ Your first sentence has to be crisp and attention grabbing: you only have between three and eight seconds to win the attention of online readers.

◆ Sentences are better if they are limited to 16 words.

◆ Paragraphs are easier to read if they are 5 lines – or fewer – in length.

Five tips to help you write better emails:

1. Imagine your audience and address them appropriately, using the right tone, style and vocabulary.

2. Build credibility. Your email readers must believe and trust what you write.

3. Use words that are easy to read on screen: email readers are scanning text and can easily become bored or irritated and click away from your message.

4. People are more likely to read an email with a subject line which is clear: 'Neil, here is your requested report on how to write better business English'.

5. Use a simple signature at the end of your email – something that gives a sound bite on your product or service, together with your contact numbers and URL.

The use of 'emoticons' is no longer considered professional, so avoid adding happy smiling faces to your messages. It's also very easy for misunderstanding to creep into messages which causes confusion and sometimes offence.

Make absolutely sure that what you say is really what you mean and check your message before clicking that send button.

84

Taking Control of Your Emails

Email is probably one of the most significant communication tools of our time. But it can also become a beast if not properly controlled.

Familiarise yourself with your email software, in particular the filter function, as it has many features which can make processing more efficient. Using filters to redirect your incoming mail to the appropriate folder makes it easier to sort through what's left, and get rid of the junk in minimum time.

Use folders to organise and prioritise incoming mail. Set up folders and decide on a time of the day or a day of the week to review and action the contents of each folder. If you have folders set up, your filters can be set to automatically forward incoming mail into the appropriate folder, leaving only messages that don't fall into a pre-set folder in your inbox.

Don't fall into the trap of checking your mail every time you see that little icon flashing 'new mail'. Check it once or twice a day. If possible, disable the icon or the 'you've got mail' pop-up message altogether. Responding to every email as it comes in only distracts you and undermines your concentration.

Make a decision about each piece of mail and act on it at once. When reviewing your incoming mail, the first decision you need to make is whether to open it at all. Some messages you can safely delete without bothering to open, as they will obviously be unsolicited. Be wary of opening attachments unless you know where they have come from – they are a good way of catching a virus.

Decide what action you need to take in response to the emails you open. Some can be deleted, others you can answer immediately if the response will only take a short time. Those that will take longer should be filed in the appropriate folder and dealt with at an appointed time.

Don't forget to use your email program's address book to manage email addresses. Most address books allow you to enter the contact's name, real address, email address, phone numbers and other basic information. By selecting a contact from your email address book, the email address will be automatically inserted into the 'to:' field. This can also be applied to groups of contacts.

Control your emails and they'll make life easier. Allowing them to control you will only cause you distress — and waste your valuable time.

Author: What are the most important rules for business people?

Edwin Booth, Booth's Supermarkets:
'Always expect the unexpected. I think personal probity is an absolute key. Never assume for one minute as you develop a business and develop more responsibility that its people don't look to you for leadership and inspiration – they do.'

Section Six

The Nuts and Bolts
of Running a Business

(85)

Survival Budgets

If you're considering stepping out into self employment you need to know you can cover your personal outgoings in the early stages of your new business.

If you want your new business to be a success you need to know how you're going to fund yourself in the first few months before the money starts to roll in. Preparing a business plan is absolutely necessary for your business but what about your personal expenditure?

Each occupation will be very different and income is likely to come from a number of different sources. In any event it's likely to be some time before your reputation gets around and work really starts to flow in.

So you need to plan how you are going to survive in the lean period before your bank balance starts to fill up. That's where a personal survival plan comes in. It tells you how much money you need every month to survive.

Firstly, list your monthly expenditure including the likes of mortgage, rent or insurance payments, council tax and utility bills, life or pensions policies, vehicle and travel costs, hire purchase and credit card payments, food and childcare provision. This will give you the minimum you need to survive but doesn't allow for trips to the cinema, eating out at restaurants or visits to friends and family.

Now list any regular sources of income such as your partner's wages, child or other benefits, and interest on any savings. A simple subtraction will now give you the amount of your available monthly income and probably result in a deficit.

If you want to ensure your career is a success you must plan how to bridge this gap for at least six months. Possible sources of cash could be a redundancy payment, savings, the sale of shares, borrowing from your family or from the bank.

Finally, don't forget to take account of any initial start-up costs such as equipment, stationery and installing an extra telephone line. They have to be paid for just at the time when you have the least free cash. On the positive side, however, you may be able to claim some of these costs back from the taxman at the end of the year.

Knowing your personal survival requirements can mean the difference between the failure or success of your business.

Raising Finance

There are several different ways of financing for small and medium-sized enterprises; here is some advice on selecting the type of financing that's right for you.

Raising money is rarely easy. It probably represents a major obstacle for most businesses that are looking to grow. And with the various shifts which have taken place in the lending markets it's important to have a clear idea of exactly what you are trying to achieve.

It is essential for any business, however large or small, to establish the most appropriate type of finance they need for the project in mind. All too often, businesses apply for finance before exploring other ways of generating cash internally. It is always worth looking at improved credit control, reducing stock levels or renegotiating agreed credit levels with suppliers before going to external lenders.

Before any application is made a new business plan should be prepared. It needs to demonstrate the cashflow of the ongoing and future business, along with its ability to service the requested loan.

Where cashflow shows a short-term requirement for funds the most appropriate type of financing is a bank overdraft or factoring. Factoring has grown considerably over the last few years and now represents a credible alternative to traditional finance. It will provide a business with around 85% of an invoice within, generally, about 24 hours.

Where the business plan shows a longer-term requirement it is worth considering commercial mortgages on any owned property or even asset-backed finance leases.

Long-term development capital is often the most difficult to raise. With venture capitalists generally not being interested in deals below £0.5m there is a gap in the market. It's a gap increasingly being filled by business angels – high-net-worth individuals willing to invest in private companies in return for a stake in the business. They can often bring other strengths and expertise into the business and there are several networks which exist to bring businesses and angels together.

There are always more ways of financing something than might at first appear. So if you're turned down the first time remember the old adage:

If at first you don't succeed. . .

Asking the Bank for Money

Most businesses have to go to the bank to borrow money at some time. You are more likely to get it if you understand how the banks think and what they are looking for.

Convincing the bank manager that your business is a good risk depends on how well you have thought out your approach. To some extent the bank manager will go on personal impressions and on what he can gather of your previous business experience. If you have already run your own business for a year or two they will already have some evidence to go on in the shape of your accounts.

But if you're a start-up it's a different story – the bank will have to take other factors into account to build up a picture of your prospective business and have realistic and thorough projections. They are looking to see if your business will satisfy three main criteria:

1. That the bank's money is secure. New businesses will probably be asked for security.

2. That it will generate sufficient cashflow to service the overdraft or loan.

3. That you will be able to make profitable use of the business and pay the interest without difficulty.

There is a saying that banks will only lend you money if you don't need it and you may well think that it's true. What it really means is that there is no use going to a bank to bail you out of trouble. Businesses in trouble generally need help with management and banks are not in a position to provide this.

As a new business you may only have hopes to go on and the bank manager will need to quantify these, so they will also want to know:

♦ What your start-up costs are going to be.

♦ Whether you have worked out what your overheads and direct costs (rent, rates, gas and electricity, depreciation on equipment, staff wages, etc.) are.

♦ What relation these are going to have to your charges.

♦ What level of trade you need to achieve to make a profit.

Like them or not, banks are still the main source of finance for small businesses. Approaching them with a good understanding of what they want will help you to present your proposal in a much more acceptable manner.

88

Asking the Bank for Money, Part 2 – CAMPARI

Here is some more advice on what the banks are looking for when you ask them for money. It might be CAMPARI time...

Character: The bank wants to know that it is lending to a reliable business. So don't be surprised if they fail to provide you with a loan on the day you walk through the door. If the bank knows your accountant it could speed up the process.

Ability: You need to demonstrate experience and your ability to carry on if things get tough. It is reassuring for a bank to hear you consider the possibility of sales being 20% below target so long as you can recover from it.

Margin: The bank will look for a margin over the Bank of England base rate. A shift in base rates is what affects your costs more than the margin, as margins are generally fixed between 1–3% above the base rate.

Purpose: You need to show a good reason for borrowing. Supporting losses is not generally acceptable (this is what equity is for), but a short period of losses – say six months – can be. Investment in assets, including stock and debtors, is the name of the game here.

Amount: Some bank managers object to funding a contingency, but others are more realistic. After preparing your spreadsheets, analyse and define where the money is going.

Repayment: You need to show that the funds will be repaid. The banks may be in business to lend money and some businesses seem to manage a permanent overdraft, but the underlying basis of a loan is that it should be repaid. If it is agreed later that the funds are used elsewhere in the business, then that is the sign of a developing relationship and increased confidence.

Insurance: The bank needs security. As ever, a property in the balance sheet or supporting personal guarantees will swing it. Banks are more cautious about security than other lenders. So tailor your approach and expectations accordingly.

Remember that every application is different and will be judged on its own merits. But the more answers you can provide to each of the above requirements the more you will enhance your chances of success.

89

Basic Bookkeeping Tips

All businesses are legally required to keep accurate books and records. It's much easier to do this regularly rather than trying to catch up after a period of weeks or months.

Cash: Cash variations are the most common cause of problems in accounts preparation and often lead to higher tax bills. Cash payments should be avoided wherever possible. Where cash is received and paid some form of record must be kept showing the source of each item.

Bank: It's wise to have separate bank accounts for your business and personal transactions. Always fill in cheque stubs. It only takes a few seconds and you probably won't remember what was for in six months time. When banking cheques write the name and amount of each cheque on the back of the copy paying-in slip.

Payments to suppliers: Check statements and attach relevant invoices to them. If any invoices are missing, request copies. Try to avoid paying round sum cheques on account (for example, £500 per week) to a supplier. Wherever possible, you should pay exact invoices.

VAT registration: If your annual turnover is likely to be over £58,000 you will have to be VAT registered. If you carry on trading when you should be VAT registered, but do not properly account for VAT, you may be liable for excessive penalties and large sums of VAT.

Use a computer: There are now many excellent software packages suitable for small businesses' bookkeeping needs, costing from £50 to £250 dependent upon your current and future requirements. They can be very useful.

In short:
- Always try to keep up to date with your accounting records.
- Tax returns and payments must dealt with prior to deadlines.
- There is no such person as a 'casual employee'; all payments to staff have to be declared.
- Keep private and business monies separate.
- Minimise the number of transactions in your business accounts.
- Use a separate credit card for business payments.
- Avoid cash – bank all receipts intact.
- Use accounting software.
- Seek help and advice at an early stage before you get into trouble.

Bookkeeping may seem like a chore, but carried out properly it can save you a lot of time and hassle later.

Cashflow Management

Maintaining a positive flow of money in your business is vital to its chances of success.

Contrary to general opinion the most common cause for businesses closing down is not that they failed to make a profit, it's that they ran out of cash.

It is possible for a business to survive even if it makes little or no profit. But the minute a business runs out of cash it's dead. The high-profile collapse of the Internet retailer Boo.com was a classic example, and there have been others.

The secret of managing cashflow is realistic forecasting. Forecasts are the hub of your business. They are the basis on which you raise money, negotiate premises and buy materials. When a business begins to run out of money it will prove almost impossible to raise funds without proper forecasts.

When preparing a cashflow forecast (as part of your business plan) the first thing to remember is that cash and profit are not the same thing. A cashflow forecast is simply an estimate of when you think you will receive money into your business and when you will have to pay it out. It is vital that these assumptions are as realistic as possible in order that you will recognise when your need for cash is going to arise and demonstrate your funding requirements. Remember that lenders are generally wary of handing out more money where forecasting has proved to be inaccurate.

Your forecast should list the different forms of money you expect to receive and the different payments – suppliers, rent, telephone, wages, etc. – that you will have to make. At the bottom of each monthly column you will have a balance which should reflect your cash requirements. The forecast should run, initially, for at least twelve months.

Forecasting is essential, but it will only be of benefit if it is checked and reconciled on a regular basis. Each week or month you should review your forecasts against what has actually happened. This will enable you to identify any deficiencies that can arise when money doesn't come in as promised or expected.

Remember, it's cash that keeps businesses alive and kicking. Profit is important but cash is king!

91

Cracking Down On Costs

Every business can find areas where costs can be cut without harming core activities. But it can pay to think ahead and take account of reactions, which may be more emotional than logical. Think carefully before making changes.

One of the keys to running a successful business is to keep your costs well under control. Cutting costs can bring immediate savings, keep you competitive and improve your profits. To do this you need to examine every single part of your business to see where and how savings can be made, and to do it on a regular basis.

Banking is a good place to start. Ensure you stay in credit by monitoring transactions closely, ideally with an online banking service. Avoid unauthorised borrowing and the high levels of interest it attracts. If you need additional finance, consider alternatives such as factoring, hire purchase and contract hire.

Shopping around and negotiating the best deals can save you money on everything from insurance, financing, banking and advertising to printing, stationery, computers and energy bills. The list is endless. Expert consultants can also help you reduce costs in particular areas, particularly if they work on a 'no win, no fee' basis. However, whilst there will undoubtedly be areas where you can make significant savings, you should think carefully about the consequences before you implement any changes. Sometimes cost-cutting can result in a reduction of the quality of what you produce. Or there can be unforeseen outcomes, such as over-dependence on a single supplier who may then go bust or even refuse to supply you because you have forced the margins down too far.

Above all, tread carefully before making changes that affect your employees. Cancelling staff training or down-grading company cars could end up proving counterproductive. In particular, any changes which have a direct bearing on employees' terms and conditions could bring all sorts of legal trouble.

Whilst cutting costs is essential to your business's well-being, remember that it also needs to be carefully managed.

92

Is Your Business Prepared for the Worst?

Being prepared for what might happen in your business could just keep it alive!

Most crises happen quickly. Your business's ability to survive is likely to depend most on how realistically and thoroughly you have prepared for any eventuality.

Good crisis management can minimize the effects of a disaster. Advance planning helps you make the right decisions and restore normality quickly. This is true whatever size your organisation is. Crisis management is not just a luxury for large organisations. Small businesses are just as vulnerable.

A crisis need not always spell doom. The ability to anticipate quickly, communicate effectively and act positively will not only help you contain any situation, it can even lead to improved public perception of your values and the quality of your business.

Ideally, get someone outside your business to help you do an audit of potential risks and hazards. They do not miss things through familiarity and may bring specialist knowledge to bear.

Each crisis is different and will demand its own solutions. However, there are three basic steps you can take to diffuse the kinds of crisis likely to affect your business.

1. Conduct an audit of all likely threats to your business. For each, investigate what steps might prevent the disaster in the first place.
2. Establish a crisis action plan to be activated when an emergency occurs. Remember to take your own possible incapacity into account when planning.
3. Develop a stand-by and follow-up programme to recoup your company's good name and business.

Ask yourself:
♦ Do you have adequate insurance including professional indemnity, product liability, reinstatement of computer data, business interruption, business contents, key people and so on?
♦ If you sell products, can you recall them easily?
♦ Do you keep regular back-ups of all data off-site?
♦ What will you tell the media, the public, customers, suppliers, and employees?
♦ How will you manage customers whose deliveries are delayed or destroyed?
♦ If your partner becomes permanently incapacitated or dies, plan how you will finance buying out them or their spouse?

Now is the time to plan your survival, leaving it until tomorrow might just be too late!

93

Crisis Management

Finding solid ground in the middle of a crisis can seem impossible. Communication is the real key to finding solutions.

There are few businesses that have not at some time faced major challenges to their continued life. And in spite of the best laid plans things sometimes go wrong. Since 1998 bankruptcy among small business has risen by 20% according to the Bankruptcy Advisory Service.

The high profile demise of various dotcoms, having spent millions on their launches, is a classic example of how even a well considered and financed businesses can very quickly go down the tubes. But what can the small business do when it seems to be facing similar difficulties?

In the past, when small businesses hit trouble, the first reaction was to close them down. But this sometimes failed to realise the true value for creditors, and jobs were lost unnecessarily. However, in today's business world the rescue culture prevails.

There are many techniques of rescue, which generally depend on how the business is set up – limited company, sole trader, partnership etc. Some methods only work where underlying problems are identified early; others have to be adopted when only drastic measures will suffice.

Where a limited company finds itself in difficulties an administrator can be appointed to buy breathing space. During administration the directors remain in office, usually continuing to run the day-to-day affairs, but receive protection against personal liability from wrongful trading. This is flexible and adaptable and allows the chance to restructure the business.

For sole traders, partnerships and limited companies one of the most commonly used rescue methods is a Voluntary Arrangement. This is more of a compromise between a business and its creditors than an insolvency procedure and requires only 75% of creditors to support it.

Perhaps one of the single most important things to do in crisis situations is talk to everyone concerned – the bank, creditors, accountants etc. It is fatal to be too embarrassed or ashamed to call on those who can help until it's too late. The more you communicate the difficulties the more chance you've got of sorting them out!

94

Preparing for Your Annual Accounts

Accounts are vitally important but can invoke fear in many. Knowing a little more about what's going on can help you make better business decisions. Use this annual event as a measure of your success.

If you get a sinking feeling at the mere thought of sorting out your annual accounts don't worry, you are not alone. And although it may not always feel like it at the time, getting ready for your annual accounts can be a very useful exercise.

Even if your business isn't required by law to have audited accounts either you or your accountant will still have to prepare accounts for taxation purposes. If your business is a limited company it has to prepare accounts each year and send them to the Inland Revenue, Companies House and its shareholders. This enables anyone who has dealings with the company to obtain sufficient information to make informed judgments on its financial position.

If, on the other hand, you are self-employed or belong to a partnership, you are still required to prepare a set of accounts for taxation purposes. The only exceptions are for very small businesses with turnover of less than £15,000, which can submit simplified 'three-line accounts'. Even then the Inland Revenue may still ask for further information.

Getting the information is not difficult – as long as your books are up to date – though the exercise will be much easier if you have been using a computerised accounting package. Try to find a quiet time of year and be prepared to think carefully about some aspects of your business, particularly the reliability of debtors and the valuation of stocks. Though, for instance, a service business may carry little in the way of physical stock it may have a number of half-finished projects. These will be classed as work in progress and treated as stock for accounting purposes.

The process of preparing annual accounts presents a real opportunity to stand back and take a good hard look at your business and consider just how well you're doing and how you could do better. It's an opportunity that you might not get at any other time of the year.

95

Tax – Keeping Records for Self-assessment

Keeping accurate records will keep the taxman happy and off your back. But what does that entail?

Keeping records is vital if you are going to do your own self-assessment – and it's also a legal requirement. Keeping accurate and complete records makes sense in other ways too. The information will be extremely useful and enable you to monitor the progress of your business. It may even reduce your annual accountancy bill. Keeping records means three things:

1. Setting up adequate records in the first place.
2. Maintaining them throughout the year.
3. Retaining them for as long as necessary – approximately six years.

There are quite specific and strict rules about keeping records for taxation purposes. Records must include the following:

◆ all amounts received and expended in the course of the trade, profession or business and the matters in respect of which the receipts and expenditure take place; and

- in the case of a trade involving dealing in goods, all sales and purchases of goods made in the course of the trade.

You must retain your records for six years from the latest date by which your tax return is to be filed and in them you are expected to:

- Record all sales and other business receipts as they come in, and retain the record.

- Keep back-up records – invoices, bank statements and paying-in slips to show where the income came from.

- Record all purchases and other expenses as they arise, and ensure – unless the amounts are very small – that you have, and retain, invoices for them.

- Keep a record of all purchases and sales of assets used in your business.

- Record all amounts taken out of the business bank account, or in cash, for you or your family's personal use.

- Record all amounts paid into the business from personal funds, for example, the proceeds of a life assurance policy.

You must also keep all bank and building society statements and pass books for any account into which money from your business has been paid or credited, or out of which you have drawn any money for the business.

It's worth remembering that failure to keep proper records can result in very hefty penalties being imposed. So it really is worth getting it right!

Tax and Christmas Gifts

How do you give a 'thank you' gift to those you work with without making Christmas a really taxing time? Here are a few tips and a quick overview of the tax position on gifts.

Staff gifts. You can be as generous as you wish with your staff to thank them for their hard work over the year, but these gifts are not tax deductible. Your staff, however, can accept gifts up to the value of £150 without attracting benefit tax. Staff parties will not be taxed as a benefit in kind, providing the cost does not exceed £75 per head.

Gifts for customers/suppliers. You may feel you want to thank a particularly loyal customer by giving a gift-wrapped bottle of 'something' but this is not a tax-allowable expense. If you want to thank a member of a firm's staff with a gift, take care; the company may have a policy of not permitting staff to accept gifts over a certain value. Be careful also not to upset anyone by singling out the person you have had more dealings with; often the whole back-office support team is involved in providing that company's service.

Gifts as PR. Christmas gifts that advertise your company, provided they are of reasonable cost (i.e., a few pounds each) are a tax-allowable expense. For instance, items printed with your company name, logo and message promote your business and are a lasting advertisement. Diaries and calendars, pens, etc. are all tried and tested ways of combining a Christmas gift and lasting PR for your business. They are also popular with the recipients. A well-designed and original Christmas card still makes a good impression and is especially appropriate if you are a design, marketing or PR company.

In order for your gifts to be tax-allowable expenses they must be permanent or semi-permanent goods (not food, drink or tobacco), bear a 'conspicuous advert' for your business and not amount to more than £50 to the same person in the same year.

And, of course, you may not only be the one giving gifts — you can receive one up to the value of £150 in a single tax year without it being taxed as a benefit-in-kind. You can be generous, but make sure you are also being careful.

Trading Status

If you are thinking of setting up in business your trading status is important. Here is an overview of the different options.

Deciding whether to operate as a sole trader, partnership or limited company isn't always easy. It involves many factors including your tax position, the other people involved and the nature of your business.

To start as a sole trader you can just get going, telling the Inland Revenue and Contributions Agency that you are self-employed. Starting as a partnership is almost as easy, though it is wise to draw up a proper agreement first. You can start a limited company from scratch, or buy one off the peg, but this can involve a lot of paperwork.

Many people feel that trading as a limited company gives them extra credibility, but whilst it has advantages it can also be more complicated and onerous. However, many organisations happily work with sole traders if they provide strong evidence of competence and skilled backup.

A sole trader has unlimited liability for all business debts. The same goes for a partnership, with the added drawback that you're also liable for all your partners' business expenses, even if they ran them up without your knowledge. In a limited company liability is limited to a certain figure. So personal assets like your home are generally safe.

In any event you will need adequate professional indemnity insurance. Sole traders need to take out a range of insurance policies as much as any limited company.

While your accounts as a sole trader or partnership must be accurate, they don't have to be audited, though you will need to satisfy the tax inspector. Limited company accounts don't need auditing if turnover is under £350,000, though you must still file them at Companies House.

Sole traders pay income tax on profits including any salary you pay yourself. Partners are taxed on their share of the profits (and salary) as if they were a sole trader. As a director of a limited company, you pay personal income tax on your salary and corporation tax on the profits you leave in your business.

This is an overview of the different trading status options. In any event you should always seek advice from a qualified, professional adviser.

Business Insurance

Working for yourself means that you lose the protection of company insurances. This can have serious implications if you don't make sure you have what you need.

Employer's liability is a legal requirement if you employ staff. It protects you against claims brought by employees who suffer injury at work. You are also required to display your certificate of insurance prominently in your office or place of work.

Public liability protects you against claims for injuries suffered by people visiting your premises. If you work from home a standard household insurance policy will not cover you when your home doubles up as your office. Anyone who, say, trips over a loose floorboard and breaks an arm will have the right to sue you for damages.

Professional indemnity insurance provides you with protection against actions for damages where you are alleged to have been guilty of negligence. These could be cases such as an accountant failing to file a client's tax returns on time or an IT consultant accidentally introducing a destructive virus into a client's computer system.

Accident and sickness insurance. If an accident or sickness means you are unable to work it's unlikely you will be able to meet your financial obligations. These policies are designed to replace your income until you can work again. Income is limited to what you normally earn in any given period, but you can reduce costs by taking a lower one. There are 'wait periods' – up to four months – in most policies meaning you have to be off work for that period before receiving payment.

Office insurance. Most businesses have physical assets of some sort. These may not be protected under existing insurance policies, particularly if you work from home. There are various policies available and you should investigate the market thoroughly to find the one which best suits you.

Car insurance. As soon as you use your car *for* work rather than simply travelling to and from it you must insure it for business use, as trips you make to see clients or co-workers are considered by insurers as being very different from 'driving to and from work'. Failure to have appropriate insurance when you drive is a criminal offence.

Being properly insured is not only important, but also a legal responsibility. You ignore it at your peril.

(99)

Entering Into a Partnership Agreement

Partnerships are notoriously difficult. So what should you be thinking about before entering into a partnership?

Lots of people starting a business consider a partnership. They are particularly common in professions such as accountancy, the law and advertising, where their advantages are well known.

However, many people starting off on the road to self-employment form a partnership as a way of providing extra support for their new enterprise, believing that by having a partner they are more likely to succeed. It is certainly true that two people working together are likely to find it easier to get business and deliver contracts, but this is not always the case.

Business partnerships need a lot of thought and planning if they are to succeed. It's not advisable to go into partnership with somebody just for the sake of having some support. Unless the partner can contribute something to the business you will be giving away what may become a valuable asset for no real purpose.

A partner should bring complementary skills or experience that will strengthen your business. These might be specialised expertise, new contacts or financial skills. Whatever the reason for forming a partnership, it is vitally important that your partner should be someone you know well in a business, not just social, capacity.

If you have the opportunity, it makes sense to work together informally on one or two projects with your prospective partner before formally establishing any partnership. This way you will learn about each other's strengths and weaknesses, and whether you can work with each other at all. It may turn out that your prospective partner's expertise or contacts, while useful, do not justify giving him a share of the business. Perhaps a consultancy fee would be a better form of remuneration.

A formal partnership agreement should be drawn up by a solicitor and each partner should consider any potential areas of dispute prior to having the agreement written in order that these can be properly dealt with in that agreement.

Thought through clearly, partnerships can bring real benefits to everyone concerned.

Partnership Agreements
in Detail

The tales of failed partnerships are legion. Here is some specific advice on the essential issues to be included in a partnership agreement.

Whilst it's true that some professional partnerships exist with little more than an agreement to pool office expenses this should be considered an exception to the rule. So before starting a business partnership it is essential to have a proper partnership agreement drawn up by a solicitor. It should cover all the following points and any others that may be relevant:

1. Who is responsible for particular aspects of the operation (e.g., accounts, marketing, client liaison, etc)?

2. What constitutes a policy decision (e.g., whether or not to take on a contract) and how it is taken? By a majority vote, if there is an uneven number of partners? By the partner responsible for the project? Only if all partners agree?

3. How are the profits to be divided? According to the amount of capital put in? According to the amount of work done by each partner? Over the whole business

done by the partnership over a year? On a job-by-job basis?

4. How much money can be drawn in the way of remuneration and on what basis? This should also take account of holiday entitlements.

5. Which items, such as cars, not exclusively used for business, can be charged to the partnership and whether there is any limitation on the amount of money involved?

6. If one of the partners retires or withdraws, how is his share of the business to be valued? Having planned exit routes makes retirement or sale much easier.

7. If work is done in office hours which does not constitute partnership business, who receives the income from that work?

8. What arbitration arrangements are there in the event of irreconcilable differences? You may well think that these will not arise, but they do.

9. If one of the partners dies, what provision should others make for his or her dependants?

Partnerships are by their very nature fraught with danger. A well-drafted agreement can prevent any unnecessary unpleasantness when the partnership is finally brought to an end.

101

Contracts

What do you do when a business relationship goes wrong? Here is some cautionary advice for dealing with difficult situations.

We frequently hear tales of the rich and famous falling out, either with their partners or managers. These cases are of such a high profile that we almost come to take them for granted. But similar situations within the business community are more common, though less frequently reported.

The simple fact is that some business relationships do turn sour. The important thing, however, is how this is responded to and how individual business people manage the situation.

Check to see whether you have a contract in place that covers as many different scenarios as possible. This should be a prerequisite in most if not all commercial relationships. Remember that a contract does not necessarily have to be in writing, though it is preferable, and it can amount to the simple signing of an official order. Where a contract is thought to be necessary at the outset of a relationship it's always better to have this drawn up, or at least looked over, by a qualified solicitor.

Relationships can fall apart through misunderstanding, circumstances or intent. However, things are rarely as clear-cut as you may hope and before dashing off to the courts it's worth analysing your own part in the break-up. An ill-considered or hasty action on your part may destroy any advantage you have.

Discussion and negotiation, even where this means compromise, will always be preferable to going to court. Litigation through the courts is not for the faint-hearted and even though new procedures have been implemented in the courts system to speed things up it is always going to be a time-consuming, costly and uncertain procedure.

Early communication by all parties will generally pay dividends. And before taking any legal action it's worth considering what remedy you actually want: is it having the contract completed or is it receiving financial compensation to cover your losses?

Above all, beware of allowing moral indignation to cloud your commercial judgement and cause you to make decisions that will not benefit you. Remember, it's not personal, it's business.

102

Data Protection and Business

Information is vital for businesses but they need to be acutely aware of exactly how they are allowed to use it.

The Data Protection Act was enacted to give individuals rights of access to information about them being held by others and to ensure that people who process data do it properly. If your business holds information (however sensitive or not) about living, identifiable individuals, you may need to notify the Data Protection Commissioner – failure to do so can result in fines up to £5,000.

However, you may be exempt from notification – though still required to comply with the law – if you use the data for core business purposes only, including staff administration (of all employees, office holders, temporary and casual workers, agents and volunteers); accounts and records; advertising, marketing and PR. So, if you hold information about your customers and prospects and use the data only to market your own products and services, you are unlikely to need to notify the Data Protection Commissioner.

The principles of the Act include stringent guidelines for data management. To be allowed to hold information on individuals you must show that they have given their consent, that it's necessary to fulfil a contract with the person, protect the person's vital interests or comply with a particular law.

The information must of course, be accurate, relevant and not excessive and you must not keep it longer than necessary while at the same time ensuring it is adequately secured.

In most cases, consent is implied if someone gives you their name and address. However, if you possess sensitive information you must obtain the individual's explicit consent to hold it. This includes information such as a person's racial or ethnic origins, medical records, religious beliefs, trade union membership, sexual life or criminal records.

Individuals have the right to receive a copy of the data you hold about them within 40 days of asking. You can charge for this, but no more than £10 for each register entry.

The Data Protection Act is complex and it is very easy to overlook its many requirements, but it is vital for your business that you do not ignore it.

Choosing and Renting Business Premises

Where you work sets the tone for every aspect of your business, affecting employees, suppliers and quite possibly, customers. But what do you look for when it's time to make a move?

How important are your business premises? Do size, location and comfort really matter? Every business has to operate from somewhere. When you choose it makes sense to look for somewhere that will meet your business's needs and contribute to its future success.

What are your real needs? There are a lot of factors to consider. Firstly, how much space do you require now, and what might that be in twelve months? Many businesses underestimate their future requirements.

Do you need to be located near your customers or suppliers? Would close proximity to your competitors be a good idea? Do you need to employ specialist people? If so, ask yourself where they are going to come from. If you have regular visits from customers and suppliers, accessibility and parking are essential. Many businesses don't need a 'shop front' at all but if you do expect to have visitors you'll need to think about the sort of impression you want to create once they arrive.

How long do you expect to be in the property? For many start-ups and small businesses the flexibility of an 'easy-in, easy-out' agreement in a lively business centre or workshop units can be ideal. Often this will involve just one month's notice to be terminated.

If however, you are more established you'll probably be thinking about leasing your premises on a longer-term arrangement, but it's probably still best to avoid anything that requires more than a five year commitment.

The question of commitment is a key issue. Before you make any decisions have a plan of where your business is going over the next five years and make sure your new premises will fit in with that plan. Too many businesses find themselves in straitjackets as a result of their choice of premises.

Enhance Your Buying Power

How to be taken seriously when buying for your business.

Every business has to buy supplies of one sort or another. All too often this is done hastily, without proper consideration and therefore fails to achieve the best result – a competitive purchase.

Competitive purchasing is important for every business. It's how profit margins are developed and maintained. But smaller businesses often think that as minnows in large ponds they are not taken seriously. There is, however, no reason why they shouldn't act like bigger fish when it comes to buying.

With most businesses now following the maxim that says 80% of business comes from just 20% of customers, it's clear that if you are purchasing small amounts from a supplier they are less likely to spend time and effort on your account. But if you show that you're a professional customer, paying promptly and have growth potential, you're quite likely to be treated differently: you will be exactly the type of customer sales people dream about.

When negotiating a purchase think clearly about the prices and terms you need and the arguments you will use to achieve them. It's important to be realistic and one way to demonstrate this is to show that you have already been quoted from another source. Sales people make their best offers when they have real competition.

It's also important to consider all your purchasing requirements and not to negotiate on the basis of one order. Look at monthly, quarterly and annual purchases and then negotiate collectively.

Price may not be the only factor. You may be able to get extended payment terms, lower delivery charges, marketing support, even an advert or mailshot that could be useful to your business.

It may be that you can supply a constant stream of quality sales leads which enhances your negotiating power. Find out your suppliers weaknesses and negotiate from a position of strength. That way you will be seen as professional and be taken much more seriously.

(105)

IT – Preventing the Crash

Good housekeeping helps prevent computer crashes. Computers are a working necessity for most people but frequently let us down. Here is some advice for maintaining a useable system.

The scenario is well known to most of us – you're half way through that important presentation which needs to be finished by 4 p.m., you've clicked 'Save' and the screen in front of you goes blank – the computer's crashed.

Computer failure is common but that's no consolation when you are up against a deadline. Generally the problem is not as catastrophic as it may seem and often it is the result of something done, or not done, to the machine by the user rather than the failure of the machine itself.

Many problems occur as a result of the lack of regular housekeeping – being so busy using the computer that we forget that it's just another machine requiring regular attention. Most people wouldn't continue to drive cars without regularly making sure there is enough oil in them – or, more to the point, wouldn't put too much oil in the engine and still expect it to run properly.

Some of the things you can do to prevent disaster are:

◆ Don't allow uncontrolled access to a network – appoint someone to take responsibility.

◆ Don't install illegally obtained programs as they often contain viruses.

◆ Don't download programs from the Internet unless you know what they are and trust the source.

◆ Regularly clear unwanted files which may be clogging up disk space.

◆ Uninstall programs in the proper manner – don't just delete them and hope for the best.

◆ Have an up-to-date virus scanner – and obtain updates on new viruses.

◆ Consider separate PCs for business and pleasure – you are more likely to have problems with the latest disks and games than with business programs.

These should help, but should the worst happen, you may need to consult a specialist data recovery provider.

As a safeguard it's wise to take daily back-ups and test the back-up regularly, using a disk maintenance tool to highlight any problems — not all back-up systems are reliable. It is also possible to insure against failure and downtime as you may lose business or money because of the failure.

Databases

Creating and maintaining an effective database can provide a real competitive advantage to your business. Here is advice on building one of the most important resources your business can have.

Databases are an extremely effective method of storing and using lots of related information in a highly productive manner. They can be as simple or as complex as you need them to be, from a straightforward spreadsheet listing all your business contacts through to a complete resource which will provide every piece of information related to a specific customer or contact.

There are three main stages of implementing and maintaining an effective database – design, creation and maintenance. When building your database you should create an outline plan of your requirements and review all stages against it.

Stay focused on the plan. Often half way through creating a database you have a wonderful idea for additional improvements. It is often better to stick to the plan and leave any additions for future updates. But a database may evolve over a number of stages and it is important that it is adapted as the requirements of the business change.

Reports are one of the most important areas of any database and you need to think carefully about how you create them. It is much better to create reusable, pre-set questions to gather information rather than ask newly formed questions each time you need to find something.

A database will often end up as one large file split into many chunks on your computer. These chunks will slow down the database and even deleting information that is no longer required will not reduce the overall space taken up. There is usually, however, the ability to 'compact' a database which will make more space available. This should be done as one of your weekly IT housekeeping chores.

Occasionally a database may become corrupt. Dependent upon the product being used there may be a tool for repairing it. Make sure you know how to do this – it may save your data one day.

And remember, information is power, you don't want to lose it!

Author: What does it take to suceed in business today?

Amanda Thompson (Blackpool Pleasure Beach & Stageworks Worldwide Productions)

'Well, it takes a lot of determination, a lot of guts and a lot of hard work really because you have to be sure that you're right in what you're doing, especially when I'm producing a show I have to be very very sure that everything I'm doing is going to be right and I see it as right. If I know that that's right I can convince everyone around me to work with me for the end product and I think I get it right most of the time. I'm sure one day I'll fail but at the moment we're okay.'

Afterword

Having read this book I can only hope that it has helped you through some of those roller-coaster times mentioned at the beginning. But, inevitably, you'll still have issues on which you need help. The Business Link network, a business advice service funded by the UK Government, offers a single point of information and access to various types of help.

Some areas of the Business Link network in England have recently gone through a period of change and restructuring. To find your local Business Link visit the national website at www.businesslink.org or call them on 0845 600 9006.

Business Link work with companies at all stages of the development process. So whether you're just starting out, looking to expand, a sole trader or an employer of up to 250 people Business Link are there to help you. Give them a call – you might just be surprised!

If you want to know how...

- To buy a home in the sun, and let it out
- To move overseas, and work well with the people who live there
- To get the job you want, in the career you like
- To plan a wedding, and make the Best Man's speech
- To build your own home, or manage a conversion
- To buy and sell houses, and make money from doing so
- To gain new skills and learning, at a later time in life
- To empower yourself, and improve your lifestyle
- To start your own business, and run it profitably
- To prepare for your retirement, and generate a pension
- To improve your English, or write a PhD
- To be a more effective manager, and a good communicator
- To write a book, and get it published

If you want to know how to do all these things and much, much more...

howtobooks

If you want to know how ... to build brilliant business connections

'Brilliant Business Connections are what everyone who wants to succeed in business really needs. But how do you make them and what should you do to get the most from them?

'Whatever your level of expertise, you will find common sense tips, advice and suggestions on how to build your own personal network of connections. Armed with this knowledge you will have greater confidence and progress further and faster with your career and building your business. You will also probably have more fun too!'

Frances Kay

Brilliant Business Connections
How powerful networking can transform you and your company's performance
Frances Kay

Frances Kay – author, businesswoman and professional coach – guides you through the intricate steps of professional and personal relationship building. She tells you how the top people do it;

- externally for business development;
- internally for positive staff relationships and proactive teams; and
- personally for a brilliant social life.

ISBN 1 85703 969 6

If you want to know how ... to make management simple

'The problem with many management books is that they're full of jargon, buzzwords, hype and theory. For many readers this can be difficult to follow. Their content, as well as being confusing, is often hard to implement. This book offers an alternative: something more straightforward; a useful, no-nonsense management handbook in easy to read style. Its aim is to help you, the reader, learn clear management techniques that promote a sense of inclusion and empowerment at all levels in the workplace.'

Frances Kay, Helen Guinness and Nicola Stevens

Making Management Simple
A practical guide to the management techniques that really make a difference
Frances Kay, Helen Guinness and Nicola Stevens

'It is good to come across a management book that is simple, not in the sense that it is basic, but in the sense that the principles of good management are explained in an easy-to-understand way. Management is not easy and we all need to work on making ourselves better at it. Use this book to do just that and it will be a tenner well spent.' – *New Law Journal*

'The book offers excellent ideas...a quick reference for all busy managers dealing with sensitive problems.' – *Building Engineer*

ISBN 1 84528 014 8